GOD, WHERE ARE YOU?

BAV GELA

Copyright © 2017 Bav Gela

The terms of the Surety7 licence available at:
suretyseven@outlook.com

DEDICATION

For my dear wife, Christina.

Thank you for your ever-present kindness, encouragement and support. I thank God for blessing me with you in my life.

I love you!

Matt 6:21

ACKNOWLEDGEMENTS

Megan Davies
2 Timothy 3:16

Janice Naiken
2 Corinthians 4:17-18

Everyone who supported *The Dark Visitor*
Thank you!*

*Please refer to the back of this book.

All Bible verses are written in the New King James Version.

Books By Bav Gela:

The Dark Visitor

God, Where Are You?

Shaman You – The Demons of Ayahuasca

INTRODUCTION

I don't know if you remember, or if you were even aware, but back in the 1990s, something incredible took place; a wave of Hindu miracles started happening all over the planet. Perhaps this is the first you have ever heard of it. If so, you're forgiven because it was just for a brief period of time and since then we have had to deal with a lot of other worldwide events. Even though the media reporting in the West understandably being west-centric, it received an immense amount of coverage. Being of the Hindu faith, as I was back then, I was more immersed as it was very real to not just my family but to our community.

The phenomenon was not just limited to temples or religious places of pilgrimages; it also manifested itself in the homes of ordinary people like you and me. It happened over the course of a few months, and was seen and felt all over the globe before things returned to what passes for normal.

One of the main sightings, which were reported from far and wide, were statues of Ganesh, the elephant god, drinking milk from saucers and spoons. It had a very similar appearance to the Roman Catholic, *Weeping Statue* occurrences, where an idol of Mary or Jesus is seen crying blood, oil etc. The whole phenomena was referred to as the *1995 Hindu Milk Miracle*. Of course, the reports and observations brought forth the usual scepticism, with the doubters and cynics appearing in the media to state that the reason for the milk being taken into the idol was that the porous nature of the stone that the idol had been carved out of was pulling the milk in. However, that line of reasoning became a little spurious as the whole experience has not continued on until today, it all just stopped in one mass halt. Another reason that the response wasn't very helpful was that the same occurrence was observed in statues made from metal, wood and various other materials, leaving those scoffers and their explanation hanging in the air.

The following story is true, and I know it to be so because it took place in my family home during the time of the worldwide happenings mentioned above. What took place was so profound that it not only changed the way my family worshipped in the future, but also contributed towards changing my personal life forever.

It was a very ordinary day, very much like any other. I'd been out with friends and was on my way home. As I approached my house, I couldn't help but see an unusually large number of cars parked in and around. The driveway was full, as was the lane. My first thought was that one of the neighbours was having a party or celebration of some kind hence the extra cars in the drive. Living in a cul-de-sac for most of my life, I had come to realise that it was the type of road in which very little of interest ever happened. The only people we usually saw were those who lived there, any visitors they may have had were usually on a weekend, and people such as the postman or electricity or gas meter reader. Of course, there were special one-off occasions such as a wedding or a funeral, but we were always given a heads up by our neighbours should the road be congested in such an event. Consequently, the road was generally very quiet and, as everyone parked their cars in their driveways, garages, and the kerb sides outside their houses, we were usually more or less clear. It was not a weekend and neither had any special events been brought to my attention, so I had no idea what was happening.

I turned off the pavement and stepped onto the driveway, passing the parked cars and making my way down the side passage that led into my back garden. As I did, I could hear the quiet rumble of people's voices and became a little concerned. But I needn't have worried, because when I emerged into the garden, I was pleasantly surprised to see that nearly all the people were from the Hindu community in my town. It was rare for any of them to come over at all, so to see so many in one place at the same time, chatting, drinking tea and in jovial spirits, was very exciting. Naturally, I wondered what had brought them all together.

As is the custom, I went around shaking people's hands. They were all very happy, and when I glanced from afar, in through the patio window of the living room, I could see that there were other people inside. It was very unusual. What on earth was going on? I wanted to find out without any further delay. At this point my older sister excitedly came over to me.

"Bav, you are not going to believe this! It's an absolute miracle!"

"What is?" I enquired. "What is an absolute miracle?"

"Come here."

My sister grabbed my arm and led me towards the kitchen door, where I saw my mother, who was grabbing something for the other guests that she was entertaining in the living room. She saw me and took me off of my sister so to speak. It was all like a whirlwind up to that point, I had so many questions, I was in confusion and so I asked her why all the people were there and what was going on.

"We have been very blessed today, Bav." She led me further into the kitchen, opposite the sink. "What do you see?"

I was really baffled. I had not long been home and I wasn't really sure what was going on. I couldn't see anything.

"There's nothing there, mum. Just a window, a sink, some tiles, and a scouring pad."

"Look closer, Bhavesh."

I did as she requested, but could still not see anything unusual. "Mum, what is it?"

As she stretched her arm out, my eyes followed along the line to where it pointed. It was clearly indicating one of the tiles. I peered at the closest one to her index finger and what I saw I couldn't believe my eyes. There, as plain and obvious as the sun in the sky, were two very small footprints. They were about one inch in length, and transparent with a bit of an eerie outline. Although they were visible to the naked eye, a camera lens just couldn't pick them out, and I should know, as I subsequently tried many times to take a photograph.

I was familiar with such mini footprints, as I had seen them before in various temples around India that I had visited, but only in the form of artwork, be it a painting or some other craftwork.

"How did they get there?" I exclaimed.

"We have been blessed, Bhavesh. A goddess has visited us. You should pray towards it."

I looked up at my mother and needed a moment to think about what I was seeing here in front of me. Then as the moment settled, I realised that what I was seeing was not at all impossible. I had seen so many unusual things in my short life and certain sections of the media had been reporting on many unusual things that had been happening in various Hindu temples around the world. On top of that, my father and mother were very respectful people. They would never think about doing anything like a hoax or something that might possibly be construed as being disrespectful to the gods and goddesses.

I then closed my eyes and prayed, unsure of what exactly to pray for, but contenting myself with giving thanks to the gods for choosing our home. When I eventually opened my eyes, I couldn't stop looking at the footsteps on the tile. They really were a work of art. They were kind of spectral and totally overwhelming.

After a short while of being in awe I went into the living room, where I went around shaking hands and saying 'hello'. There were a lot of familiar faces, as well as some I didn't know, and amidst all the chatting and celebratory excitement I noticed that some of my friends had shown up with their mothers to pay their respects. It wasn't much later in the day when my mother came in to say that her friend wanted the local news channel to know with the aim to come and visit us and report on this. I rejected the offer point blank, immediately highlighting the reasons for it being a bad idea. The invasion of privacy was the main thing, but deep inside I felt that something like that could be seen as an opportunity to mock us. There are always cynics and sceptics wherever spiritual matters are concerned, and they can be quite cruel and unfeeling in what they say. I didn't want my family to be exposed to that. My father and sister were agreement with me, so my mother, after much convincing, decided against it.

Once a suitable amount of time had elapsed, my Dad carefully cut the tile out and placed it into the temple in our home. The temple itself was a metre in height and width, and now has an entire room devoted to it. Such temples are common in Hindu homes, but they are usually small - not much bigger than a couple of shoe boxes. However, some and their components can be extremely large. For example, the one in my uncle's home has a photograph of a god which is around six foot tall. The one in our home was hand made by my father out of wood. It took about a week to complete from the design stage through to the cutting and assembly. I remember being a boy and helping him build it. Over time it has been filled up with various pictures and idols made out of stone, steel and wood. All the main Hindu gods and goddesses are represented there - Shiva, Krishna, Ganesh, Hanuman, and even one local to the village that my ancestors hail from.

Following the placement of the tile, many people to this day, come and visit my parent's home to pray towards those footprints and to seek a blessing. Some people come routinely, while others attend only on the occasion of a Hindu religious festival.

Since that time my family has moved home, and when we moved, the temple with the tile went also.

As the years passed, I always asked myself the same two questions in regards to that apparition: Why would God want to visit us in footprint form? What was to be learned from the experience?

The miracle that happened in our house was completely different to the others that were taking place at the same time. For a start, we were only very nominal Hindus with a really low level of faith, so why on earth was our house chosen? That was definitely a question that needed to be asked. We were just living life as people do, going about our everyday business. We never spent any time in the main temple in the city, or hardly any time in the one my father had built in our home when I was very young. We were simply just ticking over.

For years, no apparent answer surfaced to satisfy the question, and it would be many years later, after my conversion, that all became clear.

At the time of the miracle, the very fact that it had taken place was seen as an incredible blessing and was enough to make us, as a family, take our faith more seriously and to firm up our commitment to the gods. That dedicated attitude lasted for about a year before we started to drift back towards the way we had been before the miracle. I don't think we went all the way back because our faith boost had made us a bit stronger than we had been before, but we certainly never maintained the heights we achieved when the miracle happened in our home. And changes certainly did take place when the miracle tile took centre stage in our home temple, as we all became more strictly adhered to our faith, albeit temporarily. For example, if there was any special Hindu festivity or anything important that required prayer, incense would be burnt in the temple. We would also pray in the direction of the footprints at times of sickness or school examinations. But for me, the miracle wasn't enough to just present itself as it did. There needs to be a reason for it and how it came about. God, who created the universe, cannot be silent and then randomly make footprints appear for no conclusive reason, or make statues drink milk etc. I have already told you how unworthy we were and how low our level of faith was. Neither were we seeking any miracles or special treatment. With heavenly interactions such as these, I believe the heavenly force known as God, has to be guiding us towards revealing the meaning of life, and it absolutely has to make sense. This experience could have taken me in one particular way which was to accept this unexplained experience and just live day by day with my inherited tradition, but with my enquiring mind it actually ended up acting as a catalyst to ask certain questions, which in turn, contributed to my quest for the truth.

Since this experience, and many others, there haven't been any radical changes in the lives of any of my family apart from me.

GOD, WHERE ARE YOU?

PART 1

It was 2006 and I was almost at the end of my tether. The past twelve months or so had brought nothing but bad fortune. A decent job opportunity had fallen through, some expected work bonuses hadn't materialised, and my relationship with my dad wasn't the best, something that was brought into sharp focus when he was really annoyed because I dropped out of university. I was in need of a serious pick-me-up. Then, as so often happens, I received some good news, Burty, one of my best friends had decided to marry his long-time girlfriend.

After some time had passed, I was informed in an email that Burty's cousin would be in contact over the next few days to discuss the stag party. Stag parties, like hen parties, have always had quite a bad reputation. This has exploded spectacularly over the past twenty years or so and they seem to have become more debauched than ever. With alcohol and the excessive consumption of it being at the centre of the blame. Because of that reputation, I have to state that I've never been a fan of them really, but this was going to be different, as I knew it would involve my close circle of friends who were generally a responsible bunch.

When I had received the email I noticed that there was around about ten people who'd been invited. Five were close friends and the others were a mix of acquaintances, mainly friends of friends. With this in mind, it's fair to say that I knew they all had their heads screwed on and so nothing outrageous or regretful would take place.

In the initial call between Burty and I, he talked about the party taking place in eastern Europe. The city and country escape me now but if I was to hazard a guess I believe it was Riga in Latvia. Even though he seemed to have been convinced by a couple of friends in the group that it was the place to go, I really wanted him to reconsider. I knew immediately where we should be going, somewhere where I wanted to go for a long time - Prague, in the Czech Republic. It has a deserved reputation as a city full of beauty and I'd missed out on an opportunity of visiting there a few years earlier, which had annoyed me a great deal. I was at university at the time and a friend in my dormitory was given a chance to head out and help on the production side of *'From Hell'*, a Hollywood movie starring Johnny Depp that was being filmed out there. Sadly, I already had other arrangements in place and so with great reluctance I had to turn down the offer. When my friend returned a few months later, he relayed to me some amazing stories about both the filming and the city. Apparently the reason Prague had been chosen was because of the architecture as it is very similar to that found in London in the olden days. Now I was possibly being presented with a golden opportunity to make up for my missed chance. During our chat I was sure I must have influenced him in some way regarding the getaway, we are good friends and into the same kind of things so I was sure the hype I presented, along with online reviews would have convinced him. However, a few days later, when his cousin contacted me, I was slightly annoyed to discover that the popular choice was Latvia.

Burty and I spoke again, numerous times during the initial announcement of his wedding. He had loads of planning to do but he was excited about the idea that all his best friends would be getting together overseas for one final hurrah. I tried to reiterate the merits of Prague but by this time it was too late, he told me that he was unable to do anything about it as it was all in the hands of the best man (his cousin), and that he didn't want to interfere with his decision.

My disappointment was tempered to a large degree when I reviewed my finances. I couldn't really afford to go anyway! My year of misfortune hadn't just taken its toll on my family dynamics, but also on my work and consequently on my bank balance.

The final straw came in the form of an old university repayment, which I'd bizarrely forgotten about and it had chosen to rear its ugly head up now, out of nowhere. At that moment, I made an executive decision to deal with it in one fell swoop at the end of the month. Using savings and my current account balance, I calculated that I'd still just about have sufficient funds to tide me over the following few months, providing I go back on a low-budget university diet of instant ramen noodles. Even though I needed a break and wanted to be with my friends, the trip was simply going to be out of the question.

Over the next two weeks while I was working out how to break the news to Burty, that I wouldn't be able to go to his stag party, another email arrived. This one was informing me that the destination had been changed from Riga to Prague and that the party would be heading out there for an extended four-day weekend. Had Burty had a word and on checking out the respective cities, his cousin changed his mind? I don't know, but the proposed dates gave everyone ample opportunity to book time off work and get ready for it. Furthermore, Burty's cousin had found some reasonably priced return flights and a really decent hotel. All the costs had been totaled up and he was asking for a deposit to be transferred to his bank account as soon as possible.

What a dilemma! Having suggested Prague in the first place, I could see that getting out of the trip was going to be extremely tough. None of the excuses I'd come up with would work now. I had no idea how I was going to get out of it, especially after Burty had phoned me full of zeal and excitement to ask me if I had seen the latest email and about the switch in destination.

I had been close to the five guys, having spent a large portion of our youth growing up together. From evenings at the cinema or bowling alley in our teens to partying and clubbing in our twenties, we'd grown up together, but now we were at an age where we were beginning to settle down. The idea of a lad's holiday held much appeal as we all knew deep inside that it would be one of the last times, if not the last time, that an event like this would be happening. There aren't many people I'd make an extra effort to go away with, but Burty was one of them and so I reweighed my options, only to come up with the same conclusion as before. It was impossible. There were too many calls on my financial resources. Not only the general everyday cost of food, petrol etc., but also the regular standing bills for insurance, mobile phone and so forth. Whichever way I cut it, there was no chance I could make it work.

The communications were often with more and more emails coming through each day. On one of the very early ones there was a table on an attached spreadsheet that appeared with everyone's names down one side and various columns across the top, indicating such things as deposit paid, flight booked etc. As time passed it soon became obvious there was one name which didn't have any ticks or notation next to it, mine. I'd also taken to not picking up phone calls from my friends, including Burty, as I was still desperately trying to work out what to say so I wouldn't have to participate. I knew I couldn't talk about my finances as Burty would have simply offered to loan me the money, which is something I just didn't do. I had to come up with a genius plan and doing that was becoming increasingly difficult the more the days ticked by, as the more excited everyone was becoming, especially those who were in relationships and hadn't been away for a while.

The longer I thought about my situation, the more overwhelmed I became. How had I reached such a stage in my life? I'd had a stinking year. I'd worked hard and been responsible, yet I was not getting any luck and I was totally exhausted. I'd been pushed to my limit. I needed to get away and recharge my batteries and Prague would be the perfect place. It had been quite a while since I'd had anything to look forward to and the stag party was it - a weekend away with close friends, having a good time. It was just what I needed. Such an opportunity wouldn't come around again.

Then one afternoon as I was turning matters over in my mind for the nth time, I received a phone call from the loans company. They confirmed that they had made a mistake with the initial figures that they had given me. Slightly excited I waited for the lady to tell me that it was all a mistake, as I had originally thought, and that their systems confirmed that there was nothing to pay anymore. Sadly, that was far from what really happened. As I heard her words speak to me that I was actually outstanding more than they had initially stated and they would need a payment immediately my fume reared its head. I couldn't remember the remainder of the call, this was partly due to me being angry and also I had just decided to switch off. As I put the phone down, the anger didn't last long though as Prague came to my thoughts and something triggered in me to just go. My situation was just too overwhelmingly negative and I wanted out of it, even if it was just a little while. Though this decision was a reckless and an irresponsible thing to do, I was not going to allow my circumstances to completely overwhelm me. Besides, the break was something I absolutely needed, plus I reasoned that if I didn't go, not only would I be compromising my health and wellbeing but I would also be letting down one of my best friends. In that moment and with that decision I chose just to close my eyes, take a long run up and do my best to leap over the obstruction. I think it is fair to say that my decision owed a lot to the way I approach life.

I've always had a sunny disposition, naturally looking at things in a positive light and generally living in hope. It all stems from the age of twelve, when I was taken to India and observed the hardships that both young and old have to endure. It had a huge impact on me. At the time, I couldn't for the life of me see why I'd been taken, but upon reflection, many years later, I was able to realise why my parents had made the decision. It was really strange because I remember the idea was only revealed to me two months before I went and to make it even more difficult, neither my father, who I loved very much, nor my siblings were going with me. It was to be just me and my mother.

The reason for the trip was that I had been deeply unsettled as a child. Sadly, that way of being had stayed with me well into the years approaching my early teens. I was totally restless and a magnet for trouble. Even if it wasn't my fault, no matter how much I tried to explain, it was always going to be me getting the blame. Deep inside this made me a bit of a truth seeker, but as I was a terror, I eventually accepted it all without complaint.

To place more light on the matter, for the majority of my early life people called me 'Fred'. Everybody from my father and mother's friends to neighbours on my street, even my dad's acquaintances, everybody bar my own family, called me Fred! If we hadn't moved house in my teens, then I believe it would have permanently stuck. In fact, I had to attend a funeral in early 2015. It was for the sad and premature death of a woman who was one of my mother's best friends from our old estate. Our families had been very close and when we moved away, which was geographically quite a distance, as with most moves, we had eventually all lost touch.

On arriving at that funeral I honourably started shaking the hands of the relatives and guests. As I made my way through the room I could faintly hear whispers of the audience and it felt like I was whom they were talking about. It wasn't until I reached the husband of the deceased that I was able to work out what was on people's lips. As I took him by the hand and showed my empathy through my facial expression, he looked at me with his eyes lighting up and smile ever growing. With a large beam he looked at me and said, "Is that you Fred?"

It wasn't until just a couple of years ago that I was able to get an answer to the mystery of why they even called me that. The conversation was started by my little sister who decided, for no other reason than banter, that it was time to tell my brother-in-law that I was once called Fred. He obviously had no idea about it so he asked if it was true and why. Laughing away, my brother, sister and I all mutually agreed that it was a name that everybody called me, most probably due to the fact that most people struggle to say Bhavesh. Everything was okay for a moment, that was until my Dad decided to correct everyone. He stated that we were all wrong and that I had actually been named after someone. My ears lifted up, as my mind wondered and pondered at speed as to whom I could have been named after - celebrities, friends, nothing concrete came to mind. My Mother sat there agreeing with him that I had been named after someone and that it wasn't just a random thing. All us siblings sat there in anticipation waiting for them to say who it was. As he mumbled his way through his words my dad decided to break his own record for giving the longest delay of an answer ever.

"That character on T.V, what's his name…?" We waited and waited and waited, then eventually it came out.

"Flintstone! That's it, Fred Flintstone! That's who you were named after".

Everybody, bar me, laughed. So I'm now sitting there more confused than ever, wondering and waiting for the answer as to why I was named after a cartoon character who was from "a modern stone-age family". My dad proceeded to say, that right at the end of the intro credits, Fred Flintstone puts the milk bottles out on the door step and slams the saber-toothed tiger out for the evening as well. He locks the door and the angry saber-toothed tiger jumps in through the window, opens the door, slams Fred outside and locks the door. It's at this point that the famous and very loud "WILMA!" line comes in as he frantically tries opening the locked door from the outside. That commotion he caused in trying to open the door was why I was named after him. I was that noisy and unsettled, permanently and after many years of torment and anguish, my parents had had enough, deciding that a pilgrimage to India with visits to various temples would help change the person I was.

As it turned out, visiting temples didn't do anything for me, it was almost a waste of time, but something did happen on my excursion that would change me for the better. I was genuinely shocked and horrified by the poverty and the appalling conditions of how people lived. Their hardships and struggles were totally abnormal to my upbringing and lifestyle back in the UK. I couldn't believe that what I saw was really happening. There were children who literally had nothing except the rags they stood in and they had to slave for hours on end just to be able to afford the basic necessities to sustain life, while I was only too quick to complain and moan if I didn't get the latest toy or game. It made me not only think and re-examine my life, but also my attitude to life and those around me. I started counting my blessings and not taking everything for granted. I became more appreciative of what I had.

I freely admit that after the India experience my views went over the top on occasion and because I went so far the other way, I took to looking at the positive in absolutely everything, always comparing what negative things I heard or saw to the poor street kids I had encountered many years earlier. I became more aware of all the horrible and unjust things happening to people around the world that didn't touch directly upon my life, but which made me give thanks every day. That mode of thought started to govern my whole life.

In fact, it was through seeing those things in India, as well as other injustices in England and the world over, be they in person or on television, that I developed a habit, one which I didn't realise I had for many years, until my time in Prague. If ever I saw anything that was really unfair, I would silently call out to God asking where he was. As we all know, life is generally very unfair and there were many things going on that I didn't like at all, so I would make that call, very often, completely unaware. Sometimes silently in my mind and sometimes verbally, just loud enough for it to be out there in the world, but quietly enough so that no one else would notice. If I was outside, I would take the opportunity to look up at the sky and enquire. Poverty - "God, where are you?" Injustice - "God, where are you?" Death - "God, where are you?" upset people, abuse, sad family members etc - "God, where are you?" It became a real habit and of such a second nature that I literally didn't realise I was going through that routine nearly all the time.

I didn't calm down straight away after my trip to India. It was a gradual process that crept up on me. For example, I found myself not complaining anymore and slowly but surely my attitude to life evolved for the better. I would think, *How can I*

complain about things when I have a tap of running water in my kitchen, while there are kids out there who have to walk miles to scoop a bucket of filthy water from what's left of a drying pond?
But back to my story.

My friends eventually got hold of me and confirmed that they had booked the hotel and their tickets. However, they also said that the deposit booking time for the hotel was over and that needed to be paid in full and I'd have to sort out my flights by myself. That last bit didn't sound too bad, it just meant that if I wanted to sit with the group I had better book soon, so I needed to get onto it without further delay. That forced my hand somewhat, and I reluctantly handed over the money for them to book the room. As for the flight, the price was a little high and had risen ever so slightly, so I held back, confident that there would be a few seats left a couple of days before the departure date and that I'd be able to pick one of them up much cheaper, even more so than the group had paid. My friends were a bit concerned about me not booking immediately and Burty called a couple of times to make sure I was okay and that I was definitely going on the stag weekend. I assured him that everything was fine and I would be there.

It was just a week before the flight and I still hadn't made my booking. I was sticking to my plan and keeping a close eye on the flight prices, but annoyingly they actually rose again. So I waited longer hoping the prices would dip, at least back to where they were but then out of nowhere the unthinkable happened, to my dismay the seats on the flight vanished on the availability booking system and all became fully reserved. I was really annoyed now. Fortunately, there was a flight the following evening that had a couple of spaces remaining, so I booked it immediately and had to swallow the cost. But to make matters worse, I couldn't get the same return flight as my friends either and had to settle for one that returned late in the evening, whereas theirs returned earlier in the day. With this additional nonsense I was now looking forward to getting away more than ever.

As scheduled, my friends went off the day before me and while I anticipated my trip, they sent loads of text messages letting me know what a good time they were having and why it was going to be an epic weekend. Another friend of mine, Atour, drove me to the airport and agreed to collect me on my return. He was a Christian and we had discussed the case of God on many occasions, always agreeing and concluding that there was a divine being in the universe who was the Creator of everything and that at the base level they represented love.

It wasn't hard for me to fathom really. When I consider the way life forms and the wonder of nature, together with when I look up into the sky at night and see its sheer splendour and magnitude, I just know it. But for me, there is also something more on a personal level. From a young age, I have just known that there has been something with me, watching over me and looking out for me. I have had so many near-death experiences in my life, that I have always known something was out there but I just couldn't explain it. That isn't to say that I have been given any special treatment or had an exclusive gift bestowed upon me. On the contrary, I was brought up in a tough estate and being the only South Asian boy (other than my brother) didn't help me one bit. I just knew back then that there was some kind of presence that felt the pain and suffering that I faced and that it was waiting for me to acknowledge it. I didn't quite know what it was, but it was there and I was respectful of it.

However, I was never happy with the commonly accepted depictions of Jesus. I found Him difficult to accept. I felt that many Christians were hypocritical and that it was a bit strange that God should have a Son who performed good works on Earth, but couldn't save himself from his doom. But knowing what I know now, I realise that modern-day Christianity is subject to a lot of mockery and that, as a society, we are being subconsciously indoctrinated with contempt, if not hatred, for this innocent young man. We are happy to celebrate Christmas and Easter and to attend church for a wedding, but other than that, it appears strange that in a time of the world's current state looking uncertain, society is just not interested in digging deeper.

As I look around me, I see a total onslaught against Christian values. Movies in particular seem to specialise in cheap digs, as do many other forms of popular modern culture, such as comedy, music and television. Once-revered institutions and political parties are also guilty. There seems to be some kind of coordinated attack, both directly and indirectly, on the very tenets of Christianity. Attacks on creation, marriage etc. are all direct attacks on God.

I've known Atour since primary school, where we became firm friends. He was also affiliated to the stag party even though he wasn't going along with us. In fact, one of the friends going to Prague, Leon, had also been part of our little gang at primary school. Atour had sadly developed mental health issues in his mid-twenties and felt he had been somewhat cruelly cast to one side. Although he felt this way I could argue the case for the other side also, as on a few occasions, he decided not to take his medicines and as a result, a lot of nightmare problems occurred. Nonetheless, I still love him dearly. I knew his family quite well and he had been struggling even more so ever since the death of his mother. He had been invited to Prague, but had politely declined, much to the relief of all parties involved, including himself, as he was taking his health seriously and I assumed that it was probably best for him to avoid going due to all the partying that awaited us.

As we arrived at the airport, my conscious started nagging me about the problems I had not only left behind, but which were probably going to be a whole lot worse in the very near future. I firmly shut it out and turned my thoughts to the enjoyable holiday that lay ahead. The five of us in the group who were all very good friends had been buddies since a very early age, but due to work and life commitments, the meet ups had unfortunately become more and more infrequent. That's life, I suppose. This was our chance to really catch up and make up for lost time.

The flight out was pretty straight forward, no

surprises - and my mind was concentrated fully on meeting my friends and watching the 2006 World Cup final between Italy and France, in Berlin, which was taking place that very night. As per usual, there was a tremendous buzz around the world for this particular tournament and to my understanding; it is the final that attracted one of the largest audiences for a sporting event of all time. The favourites Brazil, had failed to reach the final as had the host nation Germany, who had been on a fantastic run as they went through the whole thing undefeated, only to lose in the semi-finals, in extra time, with two very late Italian goals breaking German hearts. The final was set between two titans of the international footballing world and there was no escaping it, as the flags and t-shirts were out in full force wherever you went.

After touch down, I grabbed my suitcase and hailed a taxi to my hotel. The volume of traffic was unbelievable and the drive took a good forty minutes, whereas on a normal day it would've been about twenty minutes tops. Along the way I messaged Leon, who advised me where to go to meet the group, as they'd found a bar a few streets away from the hotel.

The hotel was quite unique and of a pretty decent standard. Anyone who has been to the Czech Republic will tell you that the place is really picturesque. It's something very special, being very periodic but well maintained. It is that which sets the backdrop and creates the distinctive atmosphere of that beautiful city. The hotel was fully in keeping with that. After the receptionist had given me my key and a brief rundown on all the usual things, such as the location of the hotel restaurant and bar. I took my keycard and went up to my room and unshackled myself of my suitcase. There were two beds and even though I already knew, I could tell from the possessions unpacked that I'd be sharing with my friend Danny. Without wasting any more time, I freshened up after my journey, got changed and headed out to meet my friends.

On leaving, Leon texted me to say he would leave the other guys momentarily and meet me midway between the hotel and the bar which they were at. But my first port of call was a cash machine, which brought back thoughts of being reckless and irresponsible. However, I reasoned that whatever was going to happen was out of my hands. I made sure of that by withdrawing every last thing that I had and combined it with the massive withdrawal that I had from my bank back in the U.K. All of which should nicely tie me over through my holiday. Consequently, I quickly dismissed any negative thoughts rumbling around in my brain and decided that now I was in Prague, I was going to enjoy every single minute of it.

My decision to be carefree was helped by a beaming smile that I'd not seen in a while approaching from the other end of the street. As promised in his most recent text, it was Leon. He had been one of my best friends when we were growing up, but as with the other members of the group, we had lost touch over the years. Such are the pains and perils of growing older and more mature. The weekend in Prague was going to be a wonderful opportunity to reconnect. As we approached one another we opened arms and heartily embraced. It was great to see Leon and I knew the feeling was mutual.

We chatted animatedly as we made our way towards the bar, cramming in as much essential information about our respective lives as we could manage in a couple of minutes. By the time we reached the bar, I'd already succumbed to the infectious buzz of Leon's excitement. The bar, like so many others, appeared to be down one of the back streets, and as we entered, I was greeted with a massive roar of welcome. While we high-fived, hugged and raised the noise level a good few notches, the rest of the bar went silent for a moment as the other patrons turned to see what had caused all the commotion. But a few seconds after they had judged the situation, they turned back to their own conversations, drinks and the TV screens in anticipation of the match. I knew at once that I had made the right decision and any thoughts of the UK or my problems didn't enter my mind from that moment onwards. This was going to be a weekend to end all weekends and to never be forgotten.

With the drink flowing freely, we engaged in conversation. What started out as serious chat concerning our lives soon gave way to more light-hearted banter. Then it was time for the football on the screens.

The match itself was so-so. While many drinkers shouted encouragement or disparaging comments at the players, others seemed to be content to occasionally glance up at the screen before continuing their conversations. However, there was one moment that caused the whole bar to sit up and take notice. Midway through the second period of extra time, Zinedine Zidane, the captain of France, head-butted Marco Materazzi in the chest and was sent off the pitch. At the time, nobody knew why he'd done it, though it transpired later on that Materazzi had made a remark that Zidane interpreted as an insult to his family. Whatever the reason, there was no excuse for such poor behaviour by Zidane, but it certainly was a shocking moment. When it happened, the bar momentarily went completely silent as people sat and stood around looking aghast with their mouths open, probably not unlike the millions watching the drama unfold around the world, each one unable to comprehend what they had just seen. When their brains caught up with their eyes a few moments later, lots of whistling and jeering ensued. This intensified, along with much applause, when Zidane received the red card. After that, the result of the game didn't seem so important, so when it finished, we made our way out into the night for a tour of the local bars and clubs.

It may seem that the long weekend was gearing itself up into a drunken excursion, but it wasn't like that. Over the four days, we all were very moderate in our alcoholic intake and spent our time very wisely. We were all at an age where we could drink responsibly and with the benefit of our experiences in our youth, knew we could have a good time without getting stupendously drunk. We went out every night and during the days we did the tourist things, taking in all the sights such as the wonderful Charles Bridge and various other monuments and the like that had been recommended to us.

For me, it was definitely a relief to be away from my troubles but as early as the second evening there, those little thoughts about what awaited me back home started coming back into my consciousness. I'd try to do my best to block them out but I just couldn't ignore my irresponsibility and the stark reality of what was inevitably awaiting me became quite heavy and difficult to shake off. Internally, I started to get quite angry at my life circumstances and the benefits of the first day of the weekend quickly disappeared. All the dramas that awaited me, along with the pain and annoyance of dealing with it all took centre stage once more. I wondered how things had got so bad and why I'd allowed life to drift in that direction. As always, I tuned into my positive, joyous self. I suppressed those recurring thoughts and took the attitude that the weekend had been paid for, so I should at least get my money's worth and enjoy it, and that whatever would be, would be.

During my mid-twenties I grew bored with the routines and cycles that my life seemed to be built around. I wasn't miserable or unhappy, but wondered if it was really the life we have been designed to have. How many times could I go out partying, drinking, eating at top places and then maintain the joy of partaking in such activities? Don't get me wrong, I still enjoyed these things, but was there an upper limit or threshold? Deep down, I wanted more. Perhaps life, while enjoyable, was too superficial. That's how I felt. I was with my friends, which was great and we were going out, which was also fine, but only up to a point. Deep inside I wasn't really feeling the joy. Yes, I was happy, but not as ecstatic as you'd expect someone to be on a stag party with lifelong friends. There was something missing.

The stark reality became more abundantly clear on what was one of the last nights of the trip. We were at a nightclub and like most major European cities, Prague has an underbelly of vice. We were all constantly approached by girls, who while professing to be dancers, were clearly offering so much more than a dance! We went to a number of clubs and while some members of the group indulged themselves in lap dances, I never got involved. Rather, I just sat towards the back, looking on and wondering what I was actually doing there. I wasn't being superior or pious; it was just that lap dances are not really my scene. I was on a boys' weekend away, so I had to go along out of politeness, but deep inside it wasn't the real me.

As I sat watching my friends enjoying themselves with the girls, I became a little detached and it occurred to me that I was seeing in motion a microcosm of modern society. In that we have been turned into nothing more than consumers of a culture that is governed and dictated by the powers-that-be to enjoy excessive indulgence. Like just about everyone else - certainly the people I knew - I was being carried along by the water's current to wherever the water had been designed to take me. Never has the phrase 'go with the flow' seemed so apt. I thought that I and possibly my friends, could and should be worth more than this and thus doing something different, something more edifying.

Surprisingly, given my location I still thought deeply about it all. It was bad enough that I had a drama to deal with back in England, but I found myself thinking about the getaway that I had joined in with and questioning the point of it. Was it really the best that life could offer in terms of a fun alternative for me? Throughout the evening, the dancers worked the room, trying to hook paying customers, such as us, though I wasn't biting. They were very persistent and they came round more than once hoping that we'd weaken and go for a dance. I remember one girl in particular, but only because she wouldn't leave me alone. After the initial pleasantness, during which I made it abundantly clear that I wasn't interested in what she was selling, she hung around nearby and after a few moments, started talking to me normally. She ended up telling me that she was from Hungary and that she was twenty-years old. I wondered how someone so young and from so far, came to be dancing in a Czech discotheque, so I asked her some more questions about her family and background. Before replying, she looked around carefully, checking that there was nobody listening who shouldn't be.

"When I was sixteen, I was approached by a group of men and asked if I would like to work abroad. They said the work would be easy and I would earn a lot of money... much more than I could in Hungary." She paused and looked around again before continuing. "I was very stupid and believed what they said. They were kind to me and

I had no reason to doubt them. Life is not so good here for us girls." She went on to say how much she missed her family, who were still in Hungary, but that she couldn't afford to go home at the moment as she was repaying the debt of her living costs etc. We must have chatted for around ten minutes, but then something spooked her and she excused herself.

Her story was very sad and I suspect it's not untypical of the other girls who work in clubs around Europe and beyond. There really are some very unscrupulous and evil people about. After she had gone, I looked up and, as I had done so many other times without realizing, I questioned God, "Where are you?". I couldn't help but reflect on the lack of justice and fairness in the world. That in turn led me to think about my issues that were lying in wait in the UK, and it was at that moment, I fully realised the depth of my dissatisfaction. My lifestyle and even my life had really taken its toll on me.

On the last night, we decided to make the most of it and go to an expensive restaurant for one final blast. The meal was followed by a bar crawl around the city. I tried my best to join in with the fun and project the same joyous mood as the others, but my heart was no longer in it and no matter how hard I tried to cheer myself up, I just couldn't get into the party spirit. Regardless, I painted on a smile and tried my best to appear like I was having lots of fun.

I refrained from drinking much as I wasn't in the mood, besides it would be best if I didn't spend all of my remaining money, but my desperate last-minute attempt at financial damage limitation was far too little and much too late, to make any worthwhile difference. As we proceeded from place to place, the group got more and more drunk, exhibiting the type of happiness that only large quantities of alcohol can bestow, while I stayed very much on the periphery, thinking about how on earth I was going to deal with things when I got home.

The alcoholic haze of the other group members meant they didn't really notice or care that I wasn't joining in with their revelry to the fullest extent and so long as I smiled, nodded and made comments at the appropriate moments, especially when the next bar was being chosen, I was pretty much left on my own to contemplate. It was at around about ten o'clock that we found ourselves walking along to the next bar, when out of nowhere a trivial disagreement occurred between a couple in the group, which soon flared into a shoving match, and then quickly spread into the whole group getting involved. It was quite bizarre and seemed surreal at first. I don't know exactly what started it, but I'd take a wild guess and say that I think it was probably the alcohol talking. However, apart from not being very pleasant and potentially spoiling the night, if not the whole weekend, it isn't good practice to be found brawling in public on the streets of a foreign city. Consequences can be very serious, especially if drinking has been involved.

Being one of the only sober ones there, I stepped in to try and diffuse the commotion by pulling one of the instigators aside with the aim of talking him down, but before I'd had a chance to say more than a few words, the night took another unexpected twist, and the focus of everyone's ire turned on me. One of the other guys that had been arguing tried to blame me for getting involved, so I did my best to settle things down, but in his drunken state, he misconstrued my intentions and relayed his faulty thinking to the rest of the drunken party. They were in no fit state to do any logical thinking and as a result, in the heat of the moment, they decided to leave me alone and go elsewhere, including the others who I had grown up with.

As I stood in the street, watching them go, I was in disbelief. *What was going on? Where had that all come from?* I was standing there confused yet fuming. I feel ashamed to say it now but in that precise moment I began scheming up ways in which I would get my friends payback, through some other very criminal friends that I had at the time. On reflection it was absurd really, I love these people and had grown up with them, but alcohol can bring out the devil in us, and I was becoming so bitter with everything that I was momentarily seeking affirmative action for every one of my misfortunes, even if they were unfairly being placed on the heads of my friends. As my angry and out of character mind wandered, I suddenly realised that Theo, one of the guys in the party, whom I didn't know very well, had detached himself from the main group and stood with me. He told me he hadn't been drinking much either, (something I hadn't noticed because I guess I was too bound up in my own problems) and that he'd seen the whole sorry episode unfold from the sidelines. He encouraged me to not get caught up in what just took place as the guys are drunk. He suggested that we go and do our own thing and the matter will settle down, if not now then tomorrow when they wake up. I sobered in thought and agreed with his rational thinking and we walked into the night in the other direction.

While it was good to have someone on my side, someone who had seen events for what they truly were, it was very disappointing that what had, up until then, been a pleasant evening had been spoiled, at least as far as I was concerned. As we went on our way, I couldn't help but feel angry and annoyed again about what had occurred, but Theo took the edges off the situation and made me realise that things could have been a lot worse and thankfully they were not.

We salvaged what we could from the rest of the night by visiting another couple of bars and a nightclub. In a coincidence to end all coincidences, it turned out that Theo's mother was one of my mother's close friends. I must admit that I'd heard about Theo before, from my mother, but I'd never had the opportunity to meet him and there we were becoming better acquainted along the way in the most extraordinary of circumstances. We decided to call it a night at around 3.00am and took the long walk back to the hotel. Some of the other guys were already there and I had a brief chat with a couple of them before hitting the hay. I needed to try and get a good night's sleep because I knew that things were about to get a whole lot more serious the next day when I landed back in England.

I got up at the same time as my roommate,

Danny, the following morning. We were both nursing headaches from the lack of sleep and alcohol in our systems. He was not only a good friend of Burty, the groom, but his work colleague as well. We had met on a number of previous occasions so we chatted amiably for an hour or so about work and travelling, which was one of his passions. But more interestingly, he filled me in on the details of the previous evening's drama. Apparently, there had been further tensions between a couple of the guys. It was a great shame for the weekend away to have ended up in such disarray and I only hoped that Burty hadn't got too downhearted about it, and that his focus was on the three good nights that had preceded the fall out.

As the clock ticked down towards his flight time, my roommate began to pack his bags, and even though my flight wasn't until much later in the day, I decided to do the same. I vaguely remember the main group's flight was late afternoon, while mine was scheduled for much later in the evening.

With my suitcase packed, I left it by my bedside and went down with Danny to the reception area to wait for the others to appear, wondering what state they'd be in after a night of pretty heavy drinking. Sobering up takes longer and hangovers get worse as you get older and it's not the best condition to be in if you have to travel. One by one they emerged, trickling slowly down the stairs with their suitcases in tow and none of them looking a hundred percent. Eventually, they were all gathered in one place and it was time for me to bid them all goodbye. As I was doing so, I sensed all was not well. There was definitely some animosity between a couple of them. All too soon, they handed their keys back to the receptionist and went outside to climb into their pre-booked taxi.

As for me, I looked at the time and realised I had a lot of hours to pass, so I contemplated either going back to sleep or maybe just taking a walk into the city for one last look about. After that, I would make my way to the airport. However, the receptionist soon put a stop to that particular plan. She asked me for my room key, which surprised me, so I asked her why she wanted it, and she said that as it had been a group booking, I also had to check-out then as well. I was slightly miffed, but saw no point in making a fuss over something which was relatively basic, the staff had been quite good to me and we had often had banter, so I agreed and went back upstairs to collect my suitcase. Having handed in my key, I walked outside and realised that there was no way that I could stroll around the city with my big case and bag, so I might as well just head straight to the airport and waste away the hours there.

Thinking on this, I have to admit that it annoyed me. The weekend had cost me a lot, not just in financial terms and there I was having to waste my final day. Coupled with my troubles and the night just past, it was the final straw. I began to simmer, working myself up into an angry state of mind. Wheeling my suitcase over to a taxi, which just happened to be parked outside the hotel entrance, my mood became ever darker. There was just this one taxi sitting there with the engine off outside a hotel with not much happening around, completely quiet. As I approached, the window wound down. I asked the driver, who was sitting there reading a newspaper, if he would take me to the airport and the cost. He said that he would and quoted me a number of korunas, which I quickly calculated was equivalent to about forty-five pounds. I agreed and pulled my wallet out of my pocket, opened it up and looked inside. When I did, my heart nearly stopped beating. There was nothing there. For a moment I underwent a mental panic. Questions flashed through my mind. *How could it be? What had happened to my cash? I thought there was some there remaining from last night. I'm sure I didn't spend it all... did I?* I tried to behave as normally as possible under the circumstances, giving the taxi driver a weak smile letting him know that I would think about it.

I dragged my suitcase over to a wall a little distance away and concentrated on calming myself down. *There has to be some somewhere*, I reasoned. *I couldn't have spent all that money, surely. Just keep cool, think and search.* I started by going through all my jacket and trouser pockets, but with no success. *In that case*, I thought, pushing away the dark cloud of doubt that was beginning to shadow my mind, *it has to be in my suitcase.* I'd most probably put it somewhere safe, like one of the internal pockets or it could be in the jeans I wore yesterday. There'll be a perfectly reasonable explanation.

I unzipped my suitcase and I slowly raised the lid a little. Then, as unobtrusively as possible, I went through every single garment and suitcase pocket, slowly and methodically, checking and double-checking. Minutes later, I was in despair. There was nothing. No money. I was at a complete loss to explain what had happened because I usually keep a small retainer for unforeseen events and emergencies, but it was nowhere to be found.

I closed the suitcase and re-zipped it. *What to do now?* Outside the hotel was a cashpoint, but I knew there was no money in the account. However, in desperation and determined to leave no stone unturned, I went over, keyed in my pin number and hoped that I'd see some friendly figures on the tiny screen. No chance. I extracted my card and put it back in my wallet before turning away to go back to sit on the wall. I was officially broke.

To say I was deflated would be an understatement. I felt numb and lifeless. My heart was in my stomach. I was a twenty-five-minute ride away from the airport with no way of getting there. I was stranded. I pondered my options, or should that be in the singular, as there was only one. It was quite unthinkable but the only remaining option was to walk to the airport. But the more I thought about it, the more ridiculous that idea seemed. The journey from the airport had involved motorways and other busy main roads. The thought of negotiating my way around those, even without a suitcase, filled me with terror. Far too dangerous. Besides, I had no idea which direction to go in anyway. This was a time when Google maps and street-view were an idea on a piece of paper in an office filing cabinet somewhere.

Rather desperately, I extracted my wallet again

and took a look inside. No, the money hadn't reappeared. I was nearly a thousand miles from home, on a warmish day with no money and no hope of getting there anytime soon. With my wallet opened, I exhaled and looked up at the clear blue sky.

I sat there for quite some time, just thinking. The taxi that had offered to transport me must have either had a call or had decided to park somewhere else where there was more footfall and had started its engine, indicated and drove off. I was quite alone, apart from a few people walking past the hotel and cars being driven along the road. I must have sat there for about twenty minutes, a million and one things tumbling around and around in my mind, when it dawned on me that if I was going to make my flight, I'd have to leave for the airport right away. Missing my flight was not something I even wanted to think about. And there was no other option but to walk, no matter how stupid it would be. So, putting my self-pity to one side, I stood up, put my jacket back on, picked up my case and began to walk.

As I started to move away, I noticed the taxi driver who had quoted me the forty-five-pound fare returning to the hotel and parking up in the same place as before. But it was of no more than a passing interest to me, so I carried on walking, hoping I was going the right way. As I headed up the street my ears caught the sound of someone shouting. I ignored it at first but as it carried on, as you do in such circumstances, I looked around. In the distance I saw the driver gesturing for me to go over to him. Wondering what he wanted, I turned around and made my way back towards his cab. Wasting my time walking all the way back down the street again with a heavy suitcase, I was already annoyed with myself for trying to respectfully tell the driver face to face that I no longer needed his service, when really I could have simply waved him away from afar.

"How much money do you have?" he asked, as I drew close. He was looking to barter with me.

I felt rather embarrassed. "Oh, don't worry," I replied. "It's fine."

"How much money do you have?" he repeated.

"Really, it's fine."

"Just tell me."

"Nothing!" I answered, bracing myself for a tirade about wasting his time earlier.

"Nothing? You have no money?"

I nodded my head. "Yeah, I'm afraid so."

He looked at me for a couple of seconds. "Okay. Jump in."

I wasn't sure if I'd heard correctly. *He was prepared to take me to the airport for free? That couldn't be so, could it?*

"Are you sure?" I asked, hoping I wasn't trying his patience and that he'd change his mind.

He gave me a sympathetic smile. "I'm sure."

He put my suitcase in the boot and I got in the back seat. I was in shock. There's no other word for it. Something was going right at last, although in my sour mood, in no way did it make up for all the bad things that were happening to me. I still felt so bitter about life that I was not prepared to give credit where it was due. I was grateful to the driver, of course, but I wasn't prepared to accept it as some kind of miracle.

Apart from the occasional comment at the beginning of the journey, we didn't really speak. The driver concentrated on the road and traffic and I stared silently out of the window, not really seeing the passing surroundings. But it did register that I wouldn't have been able to make it to the airport on foot, as it was a long journey! Apart from the distance to be covered, the highways were dangerous for anyone to be walking alongside them.

On arrival at the airport, he hauled my suitcase out of his boot and wished me all the best. I thanked him profusely.

I made my way to the departures, found the check-in area I needed and noted the time it opened. I had many hours to wait, but at least my most immediate problem had been solved. I placed my case to the side and flopped down into a nearby seat and placed the hood of my jacket up. Inevitably, my thoughts turned to everything that had happened that weekend and what lay in wait for me when I landed in England. I was still simmering with anger and resentment.

There's nothing quite like being in an airport, waiting for a flight. As I looked around, in my boredom, I could see people from all walks of life hurrying and scurrying by, each one excited about their upcoming trip. Some would be flying away to experience something new, while others would undoubtedly be returning to their loved ones, where they would be greeted with happiness. In my frame of mind, which I'm sure was expressed all over my face and emphasised by my body language, I must have looked very out of place. Not that I cared. I just wanted to get home and move forward in whatever way I was able. The clock really did tick slower than ever that day.

Apart from when I checked in my baggage, I sat in the same seat all the time I was waiting for my flight to be called. As soon as I heard those few words being broadcast, I was up and off to the gate, making sure that I would be at the front of the queue for early boarding. It was one of those low-budget airlines with no allocated seating, so being one of the first on board, I decided to do a rather textbook childish thing. Taking into account the departure time and having seen the number of passengers at the gate, I knew that the flight wasn't going to be busy and that there would be a number of empty seats, so I went midway down the plane, selected an empty row and placed my hand luggage on the window seat, placed my jacket on the middle seat and sat by the aisle. I even made my jacket look big by folding it in a particular way. I then proceeded to watch as people walked towards me down the aisle, but always careful not to make any eye contact, sometimes looking angry as a deterrent and on occasion, I closed my eyes as if I was asleep. As my fellow travellers passed on by and sat in other rows, I was secretly pleased that my little plan had worked, though in truth it was somewhat of a hollow victory, as the flight was nowhere near booked out.

Slowly but surely, the plane became a little busier, and the more it did, the more I slouched and the more I gave off bad vibes to anyone who even dared to think about asking me to move along. Glancing from time to time out of the window, I was stewing in my thoughts about my whole situation, becoming more and more angry and embittered as the minutes ticked by. I was at the stage of questioning the whole point of life, concluding that it was a complete waste of time. You're born, you live for a short while and then you die. My thoughts became very deep.

With take-off time a matter of minutes away, I glanced back down the aisle watching the last few people trickle in. At some point I noticed a girl of a similar age to me come wandering down, looking for a seat, of which there were plenty. She went by slowly as she looked at the ones next to me, but to my relief she walked on by. As she passed I wondered how long the plane was going to sit here immobile, everything seemed to be happening at a very slow pace. Surely these final few people coming in now were the last of the lot. It must have been about a couple of minutes later when I felt a presence above my shoulder and looked up.

"Excuse me," she said, "Would you mind moving up so I can sit down?" She spoke with a low Czech accent in a very soft voice, so soft that I could barely hear her, although I did.

"I'm sorry," I replied. "Do you want something?"

She repeated her previous question.

Why? There were plenty of other places to sit elsewhere. She'd passed loads walking up here and there were loads behind me. What was so special about the two seats next to me? It was like the straw that broke the camel's back, I was furious. However, as infuriated as I was, my natural courtesy kicked in, to a degree, and I stood up, snatched my jacket and my bag throwing them exaggeratedly and then moving over to the window seat. Then, just in case she hadn't fully understood my mood, with a face like thunder, I turned to stare out of the window at the wing of the plane. I was beside myself with rage at what had just taken place.

As the plane began to make its way towards the runway, the girl started trying to strike up a conversation with me, asking what I thought about Prague and the Czech Republic in general. I couldn't believe it. First of all, she wanted my seat, then she wanted to disturb my peace and quiet by trying to talk to me. My attitude dial cranked up a couple of notches. As I said previously, her voice was so soft and she looked like a peaceful person, so I just couldn't bring myself around to appear to be too rude, so I grunted out some one-word answers, hoping she'd hear the irritation in my voice, get the message and leave me alone. I was in no mood to talk to anyone, let alone a stranger. Thankfully, she did take the hint and became silent just as the plane started to leave the ground.

Alone with my thoughts, I had worked myself up into a real internal turmoil, but after half an hour or so, the girl started back on the questions. It seemed like there was no escape and there was to be no peace for me. The questions were similar to those she asked prior to take off: What do you think of my beautiful country? Did you go here? Did you go there? Did you try this? Did you try that? What were you doing in Prague by yourself? Do you usually travel alone?

She then tried to frame her questions so I couldn't respond with one-word answers, and if I did, she always had a follow-up question waiting for me. She was making me very angry, but I answered all the same, never giving any more information than was asked for and not asking anything of her, thereby avoiding a proper discourse. All the while I was speaking, I kept looking out of the window, refusing to look in her direction and getting more and more wound up with each question. I wondered why she was bothering, as she had to make such an effort and it would be obvious to even someone who was deaf and blind that I just didn't want to engage with her. Surely if she wanted a conversation, she could have found someone else.

She dragged out of me that I'd been to Prague on a four-day weekend stag party and then the enquiries seemed to be never-ending, yet I still answered, short and sharp.

"Who was with you?"

"Friends from back home."

"Where are they?"

"They've flown back."

"How come they went back early and you're only going back now?"

"Booked late, seats were taken on the earlier flight."

"So what did you guys get up to in Prague?"

"I told you. It was a stag-do."

"What's that?"

"A pre-wedding party for the guy getting married."

"What did you do?"

"Usual guy stuff."

"Cool. Do you know the other guys well?"

"Yes."

It was all getting too much. When would she quit? I was fuming quietly and about to blow. Why couldn't she just wind her neck in? I continued staring blankly out of the window.

Words such as "Great, fantastic, awesome, wonderful" kept coming back. Words that I did not want to hear associated with the holiday, let alone life.

"It's good to get away with friends and stuff isn't it, would you all be coming back again someday?"

That was it. I'd had enough. She'd gone too far and my kindness had gone out of the window. I turned towards her...

"Would you mind just shutting up? What's wrong with you? You've been jabbering on ever since we boarded the plane. And to answer your questions: No, I didn't have a good time. I went away to celebrate my friend getting married and to get away from some big problems back in the UK and it turned into a shambles. I went out there looking for joy and happiness and didn't find it. And to cap it off, there was a problem between us all. And now I'm heading back to England to face some other seriously big problems. So, to answer your question, no, I didn't have a good time, so just leave me alone! Okay! Thanks!"

Raging, I turned back to face the window. I was unbelievably angry. But not at her or her attempts to get me into conversation. I was angry with my situation and now I was even more angrier with myself, as not only had I spoken to her in a very rude and offhand manner, affording her no respect, but I had shown myself up as an aggressive person, which I am not, and hearing everything that spilled from my own lips had annoyed me all the more.

A few moments passed as I looked out into the dusky blue of the sky when over my shoulder I heard her say the following, "Well, at least Jesus still loves you!"

What? I thought. I couldn't believe what I had heard. *Didn't she take my request on board? I'd asked her to be quiet.* But then I thought about her statement again, kind of laughed and turned to face her. "What did you say?"

"At least Jesus still loves you," she repeated.

"What?", I asked again dumbfounded.

"No matter what you're going through, Jesus has been through it and worse. It doesn't matter about your problems, or if your family or friends come or go. Whatever your situation, Jesus will always love you."

I looked at her, confused as to what was going on. And then it hit me...

At that very moment, my mind was cast back to when I was sitting on the wall near the hotel, having discovered that I didn't have any money to pay for the taxi to the airport. For one brief moment, I had looked up at the sky, as I had been for all them years earlier, finally realising that I'd been kind of calling on God throughout life but had not received an answer and then I had said out aloud, "GOD, WHERE ARE YOU?! I've been calling on you for a long long time to show me who you are, but you've remained completely silent. If you don't reveal yourself to me today, and I mean today, then forget about me for good because I'm sick of asking who you are!"

As I remembered what was my final conversation with God, all of a sudden out of nowhere an aura befell the aeroplane and enveloped me, and it comprised of nothing but love. As it did, it was as if the final puzzle piece was going right into the centre of life's mysterious jigsaw. It was a very clear divine voice but without an actual voice. I'm afraid that my limited vocabulary cannot express exactly what was going on, except to say that it was unreal, very personal and euphoric. For that moment I felt that I had been transported to a different level of existence. All my problems seemed to vanish from my mind and I experienced a feeling of complete and utter fulfillment and joy. I was so happy. I was in a state of awe. God's love for me felt so total and unconditional. In short, it was the most amazing experience that I have ever had in my life. To try and verbalise the experience is really a disservice to God and the reader of this. I know that what I have given you here is inadequate, but I just cannot describe it. The personal nature of it was incredible. But I was in absolutely no doubt that it was the truth and that it was an answer to all my prayers. I felt so unworthy. It was such a humbling privilege. All of a sudden everything made absolute sense. Of course God was Jesus! All those many years I unknowingly pleaded on behalf of people who were suffering and struggling through their lives that who else could answer, other than Jesus, the man of sorrows. Having given up His throne and live a life as an impoverished man on Earth. And having been through tremendous suffering, was able to succeed and make a pathway for us to escape. It made perfect sense, who other than God Himself to come and rescue His own creation.

The Czech girl smiled at me, which was more than I deserved after my terrible behaviour towards her. She talked to me and I tried my best to listen to what she was saying, but I was so completely blown away by what had just happened. I couldn't get around the generosity of what God had shown me, the chief of all sinners.

Quite some time passed before I was able to come down from my euphoria, and the reason for me doing so was that an idea popped into my mind. One which was to make me sober up quite fast. *"This world is predominantly Christian and I've just visited a Christian country, what just happened could actually be a major coincidence."* It wasn't easy for me to think that, as I really knew what I'd just experienced and it was the truth manifested, but it was as if a battle was now taking place in the face of this incredible miracle and it was taking place in my mind. For some reason, I was now looking for an excuse for all this wonderful news not to be true. The thought of it all just being a coincidence had just appeared in my mind, so my reasoning it out could well be the disposition of my subconscious not really wanting to have a need of any personal/tangible God in my life.

Whilst this girl continued talking to me about the life and times of Jesus Christ, I began to secretly sit up and was about to contemplate on the idea that this was all but a coming together of nothingness. I hadn't verbalised the disbelief in that moment, but at that precise instance something truly incredible happened. Suddenly, out of nowhere, a man from the row of seats in front of me stood up, turned around and thrust his hand through the gap between the seats and grabbed my arm and he whispered to me, "Hey, buddy. I'm sorry, I don't know you but I hope you don't mind, I was just sitting here quietly praying and I have just been impressed to tell you that Jesus Christ is real and that He loves you very much." He then sat back down. It was so random and out of the blue. It was completely unbelievable. The slowly dismantling puzzle was back together again with the final piece firmly placed-in permanently. To say I was happy again would be an understatement.

Over the course of the remainder of the flight, I connected well with the girl, and she is now one of my good friends. Her name is Larissa, and I am ever so grateful to God for sending her to me. I asked her about her faith and background and she told me that she was actually a Messianic Jew, which is a Jew who believes that Jesus is the Messiah.

Not long after the plane landed, we queued up at passport control. Larissa and I were still talking quite animatedly. As we chatted, I glanced ahead of us in the line and saw the man a short distance away, who had stood up and told me about Jesus. I made it my firm intention right there and then to thank him and get his name as soon as we'd been okayed to enter the country. But when we eventually made our way through to the baggage reclaim area, I couldn't see him. I looked and looked, but there was no sign of him. It appeared that everyone else from my flight was there apart from him. I guessed that he must not have had a suitcase in the hold and had just gone ahead and exited the airport. As for Larissa and I, we were both going to different destinations.

Just as we were about to part, she said she had something important to tell me.

"Before I got on the flight today, I had been in deep prayer. I've been going through some bad times myself recently and so I was praying to God, not to resolve the problems in my life, but to ask Him to use me to make an impact in someone else's life. I was desperate for God to show another soul the truth and so I asked Him to guide me today more than ever before. When I got onto the plane, I walked by the passengers row by row. As I approached you, I felt a deep conviction to sit down next to you, however I saw your face and could tell you were not in the mood for company, so I ignored the notion and walked right by. But as I walked a little further on down the aisle I was stopped in my tracks, out of nowhere I felt a still small voice say to me, "No, go back and sit next to him!."

At that point, I could see my friend Atour approaching. True to his word, he'd come to pick me up. Larissa and I said goodbye and he greeted me with a hug, which I returned.

"You were right," I told him. "Jesus is God!"
He looked at me so very happy and smiled, "I've been praying for you for a long time, Bhavesh."

Following the experience, I reflected on why

God had taken so long to answer me. I realised that the situation was just the way of life. In order to accept God, you have to surrender any preconceived ideas about Him. Which means when He appears, accepting Him as He is. I have always been a truth seeker and it was the truth that led me to God. I didn't fully comprehend it up until the moment when I made my final call on Him, that I would never have really accepted Him at any other time or in any other fashion. I had no real respect for Christians or Jesus for that matter. It was a joke of a religion, completely hypocritical. Thankfully, He never gave up on me. He isn't pushy in that way. We have to be accepting of truth over tradition. When we ask it may not come with a flashing neon sign, loud music and a chorus line of singers, but maybe in a more subtle form, and definitely in a personal way.

It was not long after that experience in the sky that my life started to change for the better. Now, I'm not saying that if you believe in Jesus, your life will be a bed of roses and that nothing untoward will ever happen again. That would be unrealistic. Yes, you will still get into all manner of scrapes and unpleasant situations - that's life - but your personal relationship with Jesus will enable you to come through to face another day, chastened, wiser and relatively unscathed, with a positive fix on the future. Pain is part of growing and a preparation for the afterlife. It is something we all must suffer, just like the Lord Jesus Christ did when He was nailed to the cross. Just because you have a bad day, it doesn't mean Jesus has abandoned you. He hasn't. He'll keep you safe and guide you towards goodness in all manner of ways that are not obvious to the human psyche, if you allow Him into your life.

GOD, WHERE ARE YOU?

Part 2

During the early days of my brand new beliefs, some very unusual things started happening to me. At least, they were unusual when compared with how my life had been up until that time. My luck changed for the better and opportunities started presenting themselves to me in all walks of life, enabling me to start addressing and taking down the problems that had beset me before I went to Prague. Needless to say, I was very happy about it. I didn't fully understand what was behind all those positive things, only assuming that as I now knew the true God in Heaven, I was being rewarded in some way.

In terms of worship, I wasn't doing anything differently. I'd simply taken off my Hindu hat and replaced it with a Christian one and continued to do what I usually did in everyday life. All the Christian friends that I had grown up with were doing pretty much the norm: drinking, smoking, partying and engaging in the typically accepted life indulgences of a modern western society. I just followed suit. I was basically the same person, but now I believed in Jesus.

It had been my desire to work in the film industry from an early age, having caught the bug at school when I was asked to orchestrate a play with four other members of my class. My dedication towards school work was highly questionable, but the play was something exciting and different. It was a challenge that would tap into my creative resources and it filled me with an enthusiasm for school that had long been absent. I took it upon myself to not only organise the group, but also to write the story and direct it. The response I got after we presented it to the school was truly amazing and even my strict drama class teacher, Mrs Laing, commended me, something she hadn't done before, ever. The classroom comedian did well. I certainly surprised a lot of people who thought I was only interested in having fun and a laugh. It was a massive ego boost. I was being appreciated for my inventiveness, innovation and imagination. People kept approaching me after the show telling me how much they'd enjoyed it. I was finally happy, doing this kind of school work.

Obviously, many years had passed since school but the desire was still there. It had taken a revival, not long after I'd dropped out of university and after my experience in the aeroplane, for me to decide to enroll into a short filmmaking course. Whilst doing an office job, I would drive once a week to attend film school to learn what I could. With a few friends I had made on the course we decided to setup our own, small production company with an aim to enter projects into short film festivals. During that time, we had much success sweeping up prizes at U.K award ceremonies, but it just wasn't enough for me. I felt like I was already playing catch up in life so I was eagerly hoping for more of a change.

So it was a great surprise and shock when an old friend rang me up one day and asked if I would be interested in doing some short-term extra work at Pinewood Studios, a world-famous and iconic British movie studio. They were looking for people to make up the numbers, so had requested those already on the roster to ask friends, relatives etc. if they'd be interested in taking part. I jumped at the chance, not so much because I wanted to act in movies, albeit in a very minor way, but for the experience. The work was for a couple of months and was great fun. I gained some very valuable insights and made a lot of friends along the way. To be honest, once the initial thrill of being on set wore off, it was quite boring, as a lot of the time was spent just sitting around and waiting. It also felt a little strange to me at times because we got paid for doing pretty much nothing.

Every morning, we would have to check in at around 6:30am with our department. Each of the sub-departments, such as costume, makeup etc., for background artists, would be briefed in one massive marquee on the day's activities and requirements, along with a general motivation talk. Once a week, on the Monday, the briefing would take place with someone from management overseeing matters or having something to say. The rest of the week was just typical. After the initial briefing, we would be all sent into our separate areas to await the call for when we were required on set.

One Monday, towards the end of the month, I arrived as normal, but couldn't find my friend or any of the new friends I had made, so I just stood to the side, waiting for the briefing to begin. While I was doing so, I noticed another guy, scruffy-looking, standing by himself nearby, so I initiated a conversation with him. We hit it off straight away and I told him a joke, which he seemed to find amusing. All in all, he seemed to be quite a friendly guy. Shortly after a while, the briefing took place and afterwards everyone went their own way and resumed their usual places.

The following day, I turned up for the briefing and noticed the man I'd been chatting to the previous morning standing next to the people who were there to make the day's announcements. I hadn't realised that he had some kind of influence around the studio. Had I done so, I probably wouldn't have approached him in the manner in which I did. With the briefing almost over, he stepped up to the centre and said, "Just one thing before you all go. Where's Bav? Has anybody seen him?" The announcement hit me. My first thought was that I was in trouble because of my joke, which I'd said the previous day, although I couldn't for the life of me think what could be wrong with it. There were a huge number of people there, and I thought that whatever was going to be said next would be hugely embarrassing, so I raised my hand and said, "Yes, I'm here," and made my way down to the front.

"Ah, Bav," he said upon seeing me. "Come here."

I walked over to him, wondering if I'd

offended him.

"You'll be working with me today. Is that okay?"

What? I couldn't believe my ears. I was expecting the worst, possibly even being fired, but instead I was being invited to work with the guy, whoever he was. It was such a relief. "Yes, sure," I said.

To cut a long story short, the man told me he was an assistant director and worked mainly in and around the on-screen action.

"What would you like me to do?" I asked.

"Nothing major. You'll just be helping me with bits and pieces on the set."

I was thrilled. The job actually entailed helping to move small things around, but most of the time, I was just watching the live action taking place in front of the cameras, seeing the actors and actresses up close and observing the director and his assistants running through their tasks. At lunchtime, everyone who I'd been working with before wanted to know exactly what I'd been doing. To them, I was rubbing shoulders with the rich and famous - the kings of the earth - and they wanted in.

My employment period ended not long after, but together with another couple of people, I was asked if I would like to stay longer, for the duration of the filming that they were doing there before they wrapped up and took the remainder of the filming overseas. I didn't hesitate for one moment and was only too pleased and eager to accept.

One day, I found myself working very close to Sir Ben Kingsley, a man I admired a great deal. He is still to this time, widely regarded as being one of the best actors on the planet. I couldn't believe my good fortune. I really was living the dream. Watching the team going through their paces was great and unlike the director, I was more than happy when they had to retake scenes, sometimes going into double figures to get the right shot, as it meant I could chat with this icon and watch the drama unfold many times over. I was literally watching a movie, live, and it was basically what I did all day. After lunch, we would return to our positions and wait while the technical crew sorted out various matters and then it was on with filming.

On one particular day, I was in a complete state of shock when Sir Ben Kingsley gave me an acting masterclass. He had opened conversation with me as the crew made some set adjustments. He was a very friendly and courteous man and quite the contrary to what I had heard from people in the food hall, who had said that he was unapproachable and moody. For me, he was a really good bloke. I told him how much I appreciated his movies, and he thanked me, asking which was my favourite. I didn't go for the obvious one that won him an Oscar, but quite candidly told him that I enjoyed a low-budget independent film I had seen him in, in which he played a hardened criminal with a very distinct attitude. I could tell my choice surprised him, but he expressed his delight at me mentioning it. Then it was time for him to return to the set. The shots were ready and the cameras were rolling. After he'd been directed through his take and a cut called, he walked back towards me, slowly. What he did next was absolutely brilliant. When he drew close, he acted out an entire scene from the aforementioned film. At that time, it was the best thing ever. Superb.

Was I loving my new job or what? Not only was I being paid well and my food and expenses being met, but I was also associating with some really interesting people. On top of this, I had made some really cool work associates and was regularly going out to parties with them. For a brief period of time, I felt really happy, but it wasn't before too long that the glitter began to sparkle less and less. Slowly but surely, I began to feel restless and dissatisfied. Superficially, I had everything but deep inside all I felt was a big hollow. Something major was missing. The initial feeling of satisfaction is transient. That was how I was feeling about my life again. I needed more fulfillment.

At the time, I thought that perhaps the solution lay in the fact that I needed to climb the career ladder and make progress, so one day I spoke to my assistant director friend in private and asked him for any advice that he could give me. I didn't have any formal training to speak of and most of my filmmaking skills had been self-developed. He asked me how serious I was about the whole thing, to which I replied, "Very." On hearing that, he said that if I was prepared to relocate to America, he could hook me up with some people/family members, a move which could open up some doors and present me with bigger opportunities. I was ecstatic. I never would have dreamed of receiving such a positive response in a thousand years. He told me that if I could just bide my time for a while, he'd put me in touch with someone as soon as the production of the film we were working on was complete.

That seemed fair, so I kept my head down and carried on working hard, leaving no cause for complaint. But as the days passed, I became very aware that in spite of the wonderful chance that was going to be presented to me, my heart was no longer in it. Work which had once filled my life with purpose and self-esteem was fast becoming meaningless. I no longer sprang out of bed in the morning, eager to get to the studio and bond with my colleagues. It was all becoming too much of an effort. In order to be a part of the team, I had to make sure I socialised with the guys and girls. And the socialising sometimes could be brutal. Occasionally, I wouldn't sleep until five o'clock in the morning and by that time it wasn't worth going to bed. I'd barely have enough time to get refreshed and changed, and then it was off once more to the studio.

At first, I relished the nights out, but before too long, I realised that I couldn't keep up that pace and that I generally just wanted a quiet night in. Sadly, that line of work is one of those closed worlds in which you have to fully partake. To do otherwise means you're left on the outside while someone else networks their way into your job or the job you have your eye on. The reason that happens is summed up in the age-old saying: it's not what you know, it's who you know.

I persevered for quite a while, but the truth be known, I was getting bored and more so with every day that passed. I'd always wanted to work on a

Hollywood movie set, but to be honest, at this point I would say that I actually enjoyed making my own films as opposed to these blockbusters. Why? Well, in a personal film project I had a hand in everything, full creative control and could work with whom I wanted, when I wanted and how I wanted. But at the studio I was just a small cog in a set of much larger cogs. Plus, on top of all of this, I have to admit that I was harbouring a terrible secret. During my personal and academic studies of filmmaking I had deciphered that movies were being constructed in such a way that they would have a damaging effect on the viewers' life. Of course I knew television and movies were bad for people generally, what with violence, sex, vice etc. But I also knew that the major motion pictures were being embedded with things not seeable to the unsuspecting person watching, but it was there and so the damage being caused was not only visual but subconscious too. I was aware deep inside that they were contributing to the decay of society and I didn't agree with it, yet here I was working for this machine. There had to be more in life, and my mind slowly started turning back to thoughts of God.

I pondered on how He had answered me in the aeroplane on the way back from Prague, a year and a bit earlier, and decided that I needed His help once more. I was desperately searching for something more, so I started talking to Him once again. I told Him that I wasn't happy with what I was doing in my life and that I couldn't understand why, as things were going well. Was I being ungrateful and being dissatisfied with what He had now given me, which was what I had always wanted? But what was it that He wanted me to do? Was it to just get on with life, living, earning money and running down the clock? I didn't believe for one moment that that was His plan for me or anyone else for that matter.

What a stark contrast to where I had been just under two years earlier. Here I was now with money, I was attending fancy parties and speaking with celebrities, and had an amazing job that was potentially leading to a dream job, but it wasn't enough. I needed to understand what the overall purpose of life was and within that, where I fitted in. I knew that I was delinquent in my church attendance and my prayer life was no more than basic, neither of which did much for me, so once again, I started asking, "God, where are you?". I didn't wait until I was in a state of prayer to do it, I'd just spend all day, wherever I happened to be, repeatedly asking the question, fully aware what I was asking.

That carried on for about a couple of months, with my job and life dissatisfaction growing ever deeper. The more I asked Him what I should be doing, the more intense I got in my questioning. I was asking more and more frequently, and even though I sometimes tried not to say anything, my desperation for change must have been showing. As time dragged on, I wondered when I'd get my answer. I was absolutely confident that it would happen and was hoping it would be really soon as I was more consciously direct, unlike the previous time when I had to wait for what seemed like forever. I also told Him that answering sooner would benefit both Him and me as I could move on in life in the right direction. I was literally offering to surrender everything.

That request had been made two weeks before a certain work day in particular when I decided to go for an early lunch break. My friend Tony and I went in ten minutes before everyone else and started helping ourselves from an incredibly massive buffet. I don't think there was any type of food not on display and we took a bit of everything. Then we grabbed a couple of seats and sat down. Looking back, it seems rather funny, because at the time, Tony was giving me some advice on eating and diet based on what he had learned when he had been a British and world bodybuilding champion some years before. Him having been a champion didn't surprise me in the least, as I have to say that he had worked very hard getting himself into shape and continued to do so.

Anyway, we were having a good chat, focusing mainly on work, when after a while other colleagues came to join us, but when I was halfway through my meal, I began to feel nauseous. I tried to ignore it, but it became so overpowering, I had to stop eating. Tony asked me what was up and I told him it was nothing serious and that it would pass. But it didn't. I'd already put my knife and fork down and at that moment I knew I wouldn't be able to eat another mouthful. In fact, the sight of food at such close quarters wasn't helping me either, so I took both my plate and cutlery to the allocated returns trolleys and then sat back down, waiting for the unpleasant feeling to subside.

However, my condition worsened. All of a

sudden, I started to feel very hot and claustrophobic even though we were in an extremely large and well-ventilated hall. I tolerated it for a little while, but it got too much and I had to excuse myself and go outside, hoping a breath of fresh air would really help ease things. It was a really horrible feeling and I'd never felt like that before in my adult life. The fresh air didn't improve matters and for a little while, I felt quite fatigued. Tony came to check up on me and pointed out that I'd been outside for about forty-five minutes, almost the entire duration of our lunch break. I was amazed it had been so long, but I guess I was so bound up with my nausea, I'd just lost track of time.

"I really don't feel very well, Tony," I said. "Something is definitely not right."

"Yeah, you look pretty rough. You should take the rest of the day off."

I didn't want to just bail on work like that, but on that occasion, it was the right advice and so I spoke to the person who was in charge of staffing and headed off.

At the time, I was staying in a hotel, which was a twenty-minute drive away from where I was working, so I located my car and drove back to my room, all the time not feeling very well. I was glad to arrive but felt that the last place I wanted to be, when I was feeling so poorly, was in that hotel, so I made a split-second decision to gather up all my stuff and drive back to my parents' house. It was a Friday and the weekend was approaching anyway, so it would also be a good opportunity to fully recover in the comfort of my family home and then

I could return to the hotel on Monday or late night Sunday, and get back to work feeling refreshed.

The drive home was really tough. I was on the road for about three hours, though it felt more like forty, but I was happy to make it back in one piece. My parents were surprised but delighted to see me and my mother went straight into fuss mode. Over the weekend, I failed to get any better. In fact, I got worse, so I went to see a doctor, who conducted a series of tests before prescribing the strongest medicine I've ever taken. He told me I had food poisoning, but not a regular strain, hence the strength of the tablets.

I was initially told to expect to be off work for a few days, but that turned into weeks, which turned into months - six to be exact. Whatever that virus was, it completely wiped me out.

Obviously, I let work know what was going on, and they were fine with it. The initial medicine that I was prescribed had no effect on the problem and so then over the months, I was prescribed many different tablets that sadly met with a similar lack of success. At one point, my doctor told me that I would have to accept my condition and learn to live with it, which was probably the most depressing news I've ever received. I was in a bad way. I could barely eat and I was fast losing weight, withering away until I began to look like a stick.

When you get struck down with the kind of sickness that I had, it really makes you stop and take stock of your life and where you are going. It brings you face-to-face with your own mortality. You've been coasting along joyfully and then all of a sudden, you realise that you aren't going to be around forever. In fact, you could die very soon. That is definitely a realisation that concentrates the mind. You become very aware of how weak and vulnerable humans are and just how precious life is, something that I think we all take for granted. I imagine it must be similar to the feeling a person gets who knows they are approaching the end of their life, whether it be from being a great age or terminally ill, should they be fortunate enough to still be in a good frame of mind during those final hours. Actually, I use the word 'fortunate' lightly, as I know a great many people would rather not know that their final breath is coming and that they'd prefer to pass away more in ignorance of the fact. Death is inevitable and touches us all throughout our lives, but it never gets any easier to deal with, even those with faith suffer deep grief. It's an emotion that makes us human, although if you ever observe animals when one of their number has died, you will see changes in behaviour and mood, which indicate that they grieve as well, but in their own way.

Feeling that perhaps my time on this planet was nearing its end, I found myself in a constant state of prayer. If I wasn't praying externally, I was making my devotions internally. I was still asking God where He was, but instead of doing so 5 or 6 times a day like I had when I had previously asked that question at the studio, my prayers were more comprehensive, occupying my every waking moment. When I look back on this, in essence I was actually doing a fast (since I was praying constantly and not able to keep much, if any, food down).

My family were naturally very concerned about me, especially my mother, and her concern turned to despair when I confided that the medicines were just not having any effect. I tried to keep it secret that my appetite was not what it had once been but a waning physical appearance is hard to hide, especially when your clothes no longer fit as well as they used to. I could feel my body becoming more and more feeble, which, given the lack of sustenance it was receiving, was no big surprise, and I hardly dared think about where it would all end up if things didn't change… and soon.

In fact, at one very low point, I must confess that I accepted the inevitable, I was going to die. I could see no other future. I started to mentally prepare myself, which was no easy task, as I desperately wanted to live, and although I felt that preparing for the opposite might hasten its coming, I felt I had no choice. I had to make my peace with God before departing.

You may think that sounds alarmist, but the prognosis certainly was not very good. I wasn't eating and the medicines weren't working. I'd been prescribed so many different ones that I'd lost count, I was feeling worse than I'd done at any time in the whole of my life and the doctor had told me that matters were out of his hands. Where was my hope to come from?

The fact that my condition had stemmed from food poisoning, something that people get quite regularly, but recover from, really annoyed me, but what was the point of such anger? All the irritation that I vented just made the situation worse. Yet it was hard to stop. I couldn't not think about it, no matter how hard I tried. We all assume that we will live till a ripe old age, so when you see death staring you in the face, as a relatively young man, it comes as a real eye opener. Throughout my long period of incapacitation, I prayed like I had never prayed before, although I didn't pray to be healed, which I really should have done, but I prayed to know the truth before I died. I was of a mind that by making an enquiry of the truth, I would have at least used some of my time on earth wisely and unselfishly. Furthermore, by asking the question, I was not just being accepting of my life's circumstances or being washed along in the river of self.

Then something quite amazing happened. From being on a downward spiral, with my health fast approaching the point of no return, I stabilised and started to improve. I found that I felt like eating and I reached a point where I could keep the food down and feel my body regenerating. My weight had reached its lowest point and thankfully I began to put on a couple of pounds. It was slow progress, but I was moving in the right direction. Although I was still bedridden, I felt wave after wave of relief wash over me. I was going to live. I can't even begin to tell you how uplifted I felt. My mind rejoiced and ideas of getting up and going about my business as normal filled my head. But I was still very weak, so I wisely chose to ignore them and give myself sufficient time to heal. It wouldn't happen in five minutes, not even in five days. I had to encourage myself to not get too excited and be patient. It would most likely be a long haul back. I had been very close to death's door and if I was to make it back to full health, I would need a lot of rest and recuperation to allow me to mend. Over the past few years, I'd been flat out and perhaps that had exacerbated my situation, but whether or not that was indeed the case, I was determined to make the most of the second chance that I'd been given.

I massively increased my praying and pleading, for God to show Himself to me and over the following week I was subjected to a bizarre chain of events.

First of all, a group of evangelicals knocked at my door. They were representing a super church, which had not long been built at the back of my family house. Then later in that same week, a Mormon couple called by. Shortly after, as if to push the point, it was the turn of some Jehovah's Witnesses. What was going on? While I was thinking about those three religious groups all making contact at about the same time, an old Catholic friend, who I'd lost touch with, reconnected with me out of the blue. He was soon followed by a Muslim friend. All of them wanted to talk to me about God. None knew my situation or what was going on in my religious life, they just started appearing to promote their views. Now this had to be a lot more than sheer coincidence, especially as the street in which my parents' house was situated was usually pretty quiet. The series of callings when taken as a whole had a definite surreal feeling about them. I began to question whether God was trying to tell me something. Was He trying to draw me in closer through one of the faith groups or the faiths that my two old friends have?

I very much valued the people who came to talk to me about God. They were all very polite, pleasant, sincere and respectful and I appreciated them taking time out of their busy lives to go round talking to people like me about their beliefs. Although I admired their dedication, I made a call out to God. I have always been interested in truth and truth only, this is what has brought me along this journey. Now I was seeking it again. So I made a declaration to Jesus, that I would not be interested in any of those groups unless He made it very clear to me. If He was prepared to give me a miracle in an aeroplane then He should be able to answer this request. I wasn't well and this was another life-changing situation, I needed Him to give me absolute clarity.

During that same period, I was trying to take my mind off what was happening with my health by watching documentaries. I lost count of the number I got through, but I can tell you they became one of my favourite pastimes. I specifically started to watch ones on religion, hoping that God may somehow inspire me. At one point I started watching a series on Islam. It was a low-budget production and had been split into something like thirty parts, with each one being about six minutes long. I found it to be a very interesting series, particularly when it was dealing with the media and the negative influence and impact it can have on people. Because of my job it really resonated with me. Islam certainly exerted a pull in my direction and the major draw for me was that they believe in Jesus. As I had already been convinced of Jesus, it wasn't hard for me to be persuaded. There was a problem though, and that was that the Christ I had been convicted of was God himself, manifested as man. I had absolutely no doubt about it at all. Yet here this documentary (as well as the Jehovah's Witnesses who had knocked on my door earlier in the week) were saying that He was not God.

I was really getting a lot from the series, so much so that it made me ask my Muslim friend, who had recently reconnected with me, to get me a Koran in English so that I could read it. I asked him three times and each time he failed to bring me one, saying he had forgotten. At the time when all those faith groups had been turning up at my door, I had specifically asked God to block anything which wasn't from Him, so I reasoned maybe that was why he kept forgetting. But I carried on with watching the documentary series regardless, as I still felt a strong pull on a personal level due to the fact that they were lifting a few lids on the dangers of movies and television.

In and around the twentieth episode, upon the screen came a short clip of an old man speaking quite candidly about a war taking place in the invisible world around us. He talked about his experiences from a time when he'd joined a secret society and had been a Satanist who'd encountered demons and angels. He was very open and humble and the things he spoke about were fascinating and really struck a chord with me because I was able to relate them to incidents I'd experienced in my life while growing up.

When I went to sleep that night, I drifted off as usual, but this night was completely different to any other I have ever had before. As I slept, all I could see, all night long, was the interview clip of the man's confession, and accompanying it was a very peaceful yet firm tone telling me to find out about this old man and then I will find the answer to all my questions. It was quite ridiculous, because my mind is usually blank when I'm asleep and I barely remember any pictures or sounds in any dreams. But that night was different. I just kept seeing that man's face and hearing the same thing being repeated over and over again with strict emphasis.

When I woke up the following day, I was ecstatic. Finally, God had come through for me. I absolutely knew it was Him communicating to me again. It was the same God of love and peace that had spoken to me in the aeroplane.

I wasted no time, I jumped on the internet with a strong desire to search out the old ex-Satanist, but nothing showed up, which was not really surprising, as I had no details to enter - no name, no location, nothing. I tried countless combinations of 'ex-Satanist Islam', 'old man ex-Satanist Muslim' etc., but still nothing. I was really frustrated. Why would God reveal Jesus as God in the aeroplane yet now he was wanting me to seek out and embrace the Jesus of Islam? I spent nearly almost every hour searching that day but nothing showed up. With all the effort I put in I became quite discouraged.

However, not being one to give up easily, I reasoned that he might appear once more somewhere further on in the documentary series, so I decided to watch another episode in the hope that more would be revealed. Again I was to experience disappointment. The series moved completely in another direction. I was very disheartened and even slightly annoyed, so I decided to take a step back from the search, stating that the Lord knew my case because I had made it clear what my wish was.

As I went to sleep that night, I had the same thing in my dreams as I'd had the previous night - that old man's face and a voice telling me that if I find the old man I will find God. I was hoping that some clue I'd missed might present itself to me during my sleep, but there wasn't one. Regardless, when I woke up the following morning I had a renewed urge and desire to track the man down. I made it my mission for the day. I tried harder with my search attempts, hoping that something would come up. It was really frustrating. As I said earlier, the problem was that I didn't have anything definite to go on.

I sat there thinking and thinking and decided to re-watch the episode again, almost positive that there would be some hidden detail which I could submit to the mighty Google algorithms, but nothing more was there. Then I had a bit of inspiration. I decided to try various forums that were dedicated to Islam and see if there was anything about the series I was watching. Surely there would be something. Feeling I was near my answer, I started searching and reading with renewed vigor. It wasn't as easy a task as I'd thought. Very soon passed a couple of hours with only minor traces of the documentary but no mention of the old man whatsoever.

To say I was becoming anxious would be an understatement, but I kept on searching. It had to be somewhere! I re-watched the episode again and again, analysing the man's words and speech, and using them for my search, but still nothing. In the end, I got so frustrated that I gave up. I was feeling very aggrieved and bitter for wasting so much time on something that had proved to be so fruitless. I thought it was extremely strange that I couldn't find anything. It was as if the documentary really only existed on my computer. I consoled myself with the thought that I can't do anything more other than to pray. God knows my desire to know Him and I have been completely dedicated, submissive and transparent. I had tried everything I could to find Him, but to no avail. I even asked God why He was placing this burden of seeking the man out on me. All the while, I continued to watch many other religious documentaries but this online series on Islam was the only one that God had brought to my attention through my dreams, so I decided to just be patient, continue watching and waited on the good Lord to make the revelation.

As I approached the final few episodes, my mind was pressed with the same burden every night. Many things were impacting my thought processes at the time and out of all the routes that were being placed in front of me, I must admit that at one point I felt that God might eventually want me to follow the course of Islam further down the road. Yet when I delved into my thoughts a little deeper, taking a more detached and dispassionate view, I found it was the old man who was responsible for those feelings and not the religion as such. Additionally, although there were many good things in the documentary there were also quite a number of things that annoyed me and I'm not just referring to the technical quality of the video production. I noticed a not too subtle tactic of promoting certain agendas, which I thought was very underhanded. I've always maintained and believed that Godly things should be done with reverence and fairness etc., and the soundtrack used in this series had been stolen from a popular Hollywood movie and used unlawfully. I tried to find a justification for that, and could only think that maybe the people making the series had stepped out of the usual parameters to try and get the message about God across with a little more zeal. Whether or not that was the case, I obviously don't know, but the illegal use of someone else's music to try and glorify God did leave me feeling uneasy. Consequently, I watched the series to the very end, all the time still having the same night-time visions.

Then the completely unexpected happened. In the second to last episode, they did a quick recap of the series. At one point they re-showed the short clip that featured the old man. But this time around, it was accompanied by a narrator's voiceover, that was now analysing and summarising what had passed to date. As I listened, I couldn't believe my ears. They referred to the old man by his first name - Roger. I was really ecstatic. It would make my quest, while not easy, certainly easier. I now had something more solid on which to base my search on. It seemed strange that the man should have a Christian name and not one that was Islamic, but I figured perhaps it wasn't mandatory to change it and that there were probably loads of Islamic converts who had held on to the name they had been given at birth. Anyway, all I was thinking then was that if the man was still alive, I would love to speak to him further about the matters he briefly touched upon in the short segment.

I immediately turned to Google and recommenced my search, using some of the words and phrases I'd used before, but with the addition of the word 'Roger'. Much to my delight, it wasn't long before his face popped up on the screen. I quickly discovered that his full name was in fact Roger Morneau, which made it sound like he was of French descent, something which I'd suspected because of his accent.

As I slowly began to scroll down through the search results for more information about him, I was really shocked to see that he was something called a Seventh-day Adventist. *What on earth was a Seventh-day Adventist??* I had no idea. There was only one thing I could do, and that was to research it.

I discovered the Seventh-day Adventist Church is a Christian organisation and quite a popular one at that, although it had certainly passed me by as I'd never heard of it before in my life. During this investigation, my joy all of a sudden massively increased when I came upon a three-hour in-depth interview with Roger Morneau called *'A Trip into the Supernatural'*. As I began to watch it, it was clear from where the clip in the Islam documentary series had been taken from. It worried and unsettled me that the makers of the documentary on Islam had used a clip from a Seventh-day Adventist testimony to promote their ideas, especially as they had made no such acknowledgement.

I didn't waste any time and began watching the Roger Morneau interview immediately. God had promised me through a dream that I will find Him if I seek this man out. For three hours I watched avidly, and when it was over, I sat there feeling completely bowled over. Other than the fact that I knew that nobody would ever spend three hours speaking about something in great detail and without batting an eyelid unless they'd had real experiences of it, it also struck me at that moment that I had major closure on the things I had been questioning in my life. I had seen and experienced many things, unusual things which I did not understand but now I was absolutely convicted that this was the truth! The interview really jolted me.

As I tried to turn in that evening, I could hardly sleep, I couldn't stop replaying parts of the interview in my head and my mind was totally seized with what Morneau had said. Having sought and found the old man, I was now becoming anxious to find out about Seventh-day Adventists and to see what it was all about. Of course, it presented me with another problem, although not one that was too burdensome. What was I to do next?

I woke up the following morning wondering

what was so special about this group of people that I had never even heard of before, so I did some more research online. The thing that really caught my eye was the fact that they worship on Saturdays rather than Sunday. I was really impressed with what I read about their views on lifestyle but held back from calling them directly for a couple of weeks. Perhaps I was just letting things settle in my mind, I don't know, but I would always find an excuse not to make contact with the church by looking online and finding someone's negative critique that would put me off. It was stupid of me really because any critique is only the thoughts of one person and just because they put it online, that doesn't make it any more authoritative than someone giving you an opinion at a bus stop. Also, anyone can setup a website and be negative about an institution or group of people, especially if they have an axe to grind.

My hesitancy to boldly go forth was also due to my worries about the fact that I had never heard of them. If they really were God's people, surely they would have been more popular than they are and had appeared somewhere on my radar before now. At the age of thirty, I would have expected to at least to have heard of their name, even if that was as far as my knowledge went.

But in truth, I was just looking for excuses. I was searching around for a reason, any reason, to reject Seventh-day Adventism. It was like I'd found this amazing truth but was now too afraid to touch it and grasp it with both hands. I was fully convinced and all the dots of life had been joined. Everything I'd asked had now been answered and was leading me to these people. So what was I waiting for?

As is normal with me, there were now a whole load of new questions but they were more about the Adventists and their practices. I knew from the overwhelming inspiration I'd received that this church would fulfill all my longings and wants.

It was now or never. I did a quick online search for the location of the nearest Seventh-day Adventist church. There was only one in the city centre at the time and although I wasn't completely familiar with the area or the street name, I knew more or less where it was.

Another step forward, but once again, thoughts started to play away at the back of my mind. Even if it was the truth, what if this particular church wasn't tailored for me? Would it be a happy-clappy outfit or one where little old ladies sat around drinking tea and eating biscuits? I know that making these assumptions is narrow-minded but those images stemmed out of my own ignorance from Christian references in television shows and the like.

Pushing that to one side, I logged on to my local church's official website. Scrolling down, I saw their telephone number. I then plucked up some courage and called them to clarify a few things. The phone was answered by a pleasant old man, who from his tone and friendliness was obviously happy that I'd called. After I awkwardly enquired, he clarified that they were indeed the very Adventists I was seeking who worship on Saturdays, believed in Jesus Christ and believed that He was God. After a brief chat, he invited me to go along at any time I liked. After I had put the phone down I was really surprised by the way the guy didn't pressure me into knowing my name, address etc., nor did he push me to come to church straight away. He just left it to me. That really impressed me because I must admit that I was expecting him to be institutionally pushy. I decided then and there that I was going to pay them a visit. I had the address, so all I had to do was to psyche myself up to step into the unknown and ensure that physically (I was still far from being well) I'd be capable of visiting them.

I earmarked a Saturday, two weeks into the future, on which I would attend. I waited for the time to pass during which I took part in a lot of contemplation and prayer. But when the big day came I talked myself out of going, reasoning that I'm quite unwell and promised myself that I'd definitely attend another time.

My mind was a bit of a battleground. I was convinced about this movement, but just wanted things to be perfect. I would then postpone my visit to another future Saturday and when that day came around, I'd cancel again and set another day. Why couldn't I commit? There was no logical reason at all not to go and what would be the worst that could happen? If I didn't like it, I could up and leave and never see the church or any of the people ever again. But my mind was not letting me off so easily.

I believe I was bothered about what those who I was close to and loved would think. Also I kept asking myself why being a Christian wasn't sufficient enough and I would also wonder why the Saturday thing. Why was God bothered whether you worshipped on a Saturday instead of the traditional Sunday?

So a great many Saturdays came and went without me taking any action, but I prayed solidly throughout for guidance and I found my motivation alongside my yearning growing stronger by the day. The annoying little worries that were holding me back began to recede as I realised my quest of my want for God and for truth regardless of what sacrifices I would make in this world. After what seemed like ages since I'd initially phoned the church, I was ready to take the step. I just had to, as I'd waited long enough and I needed to get some closure on all of this. I decided I had to step out and go, not just for my sake and peace of mind, but also, and more importantly for God. He in His kindness had brought me so far along the road and it was the least I could do to repay His faith in me. I owed it to Him. I looked at my calendar and earmarked the Saturday that was nearly a fortnight away. I was ready to take the plunge. I reasoned at the time that two weeks would give me plenty of time to prepare myself and get ready for this.

The days passed excruciatingly slowly, which I appreciated to a degree, as I wanted to be well enough to be able to analyse and assess the things which I would find out on my day out, but on the other hand I felt spiritually revitalised and more than ever wanted to go and meet God.

Eventually, the Saturday arrived. I didn't sleep much the night before as I spent most of the time lying awake in reflection, thought and prayer. But it wasn't a problem as I surprisingly woke up feeling good. I got up and had a light breakfast along with all the other usual morning prep, then headed for the front door. This was it. I was actually going! It was about half past ten and the man from the church had said that the best time to arrive would be at around eleven o'clock, so factoring in the Saturday traffic, I'd calculated the drive would take me about half an hour.

As I opened the front door of my house and stepped out on to the driveway, what I was confronted with next was quite possibly one of the most bizarre scenarios I had ever experienced! I literally couldn't believe what was in front of me and on this day of all days. My car door was bent in half and it had been pulled away from the car so that it was hanging by its hinges! I was stunned. My face would have been quite a picture for anyone passing by at that moment. We lived in a quiet area and the manner in which the damage had been done was simply off the scale. I walked over to it with emotions of confusion stirring around. I stood and stared, finding it impossible to take in what lay before me. I felt numb. *Who could have done such a thing? And why? And when did they do it? How late into the night? And if it was late, why did nobody hear them? It would have been quiet enough and bending a car door in half and pulling it off the frame is a little excessive and isn't something that anyone can do without making quite a noise.*

The car was obviously not roadworthy so I cancelled going to church and began the process of getting my door fixed. I ordered a new one, which took several weeks to arrive and when it did, I got a mechanic friend of mine to fit it. The whole process took about a month.

In the meantime, I decided to put the incident down to one of the random acts of vandalism that seem to be all too frequent nowadays. Anyhow, I was still determined to visit the Seventh-day Adventist church and continued with my private contemplation and prayers which bolstered my resolve. I decided to set aside another Saturday on the calendar. Again, I gave myself a two-week leeway. This time it was because I had suffered a bit of a health setback after the car had been trashed, which is hardly surprising, as I was in a weak state anyway and the whole matter was very stressful.

I found the wait even more difficult than on the previous occasion and once again I had very little sleep as I spent time contemplating on what awaited me. One day, on the week I was due to go, I believe it to be Wednesday but I cannot be sure, I was just getting ready to leave the house to go for a walk. When I stepped out on to the driveway, I locked my house door and turned to my car. In that moment I couldn't believe my eyes. My car door had been bent in half again and ripped away! *What on earth was going on??* Once again, I was completely dumbfounded. I couldn't believe that it was just a coincidence. On both weeks that I was supposed to go to the church, my car had been damaged to the point where I couldn't drive it. And nothing like that had ever happened to me or to anyone I knew before. It was then that I realised that there was definitely something trying to halt me from going.

In my confusion I attempted to think for a moment, trying to remember if I had told anyone about my plan and if there was a possibility that they could be trying to stop me from fulfilling it. But on sober reflection I hadn't, and even if I had done, ripping off a car door twice is rather extreme. Besides, nobody I knew would behave in such an anti-social manner.

Once more I had to postpone and get the car door fixed. Unlike the first time though, I called the police. They came over and did a forensic test but couldn't find anything useful. I was also getting seriously annoyed. Apart from the fact that I was being prevented from meeting up with God, it was all getting very expensive despite my friend providing the labour.

I prayed a lot that week, asking numerous questions. *Why is this happening to me? Do You not want me to go to the Adventists? If You do, You have to protect me! Besides, I cannot afford to buy anymore car doors!*

It was in this period of time that I started to think seriously about all the unexplainable spiritual things that I had seen in my life. These include, the Hindu apparition of the footprints, the countless near-death situations (from falling from great heights and being electrocuted to almost drowning) and the possessions that I had seen take place over various people at certain religious events. However, two things which really dawned heavy on me were both experiences from my youth which I had not properly focused on since they had taken place. Why? Well, I think it was because they were both surreal and at the time I didn't think anyone would believe me. Also one of them was extremely terrifying and the beings that were involved were certainly not human. 🄾

Once the car door had been replaced, I specifically prayed to God that if He wanted me to go to the church He had to protect me and my car no matter what. Then when I sat down to choose a suitable Saturday, I zeroed straight in on the coming weekend. No waiting. I was determined to strike while the iron was hot. I wanted to go and I felt physically able, all fear and doubt had long gone. I was also very intrigued about what was blocking me from going to such a place as a church.

Saturday came, again, and I got changed, again. At around ten thirty, I hesitantly opened the front door of my house. Hardly daring to, I reluctantly looked towards my car expecting the worst. Everything looked okay. I breathed a huge sigh of relief and went to make a closer inspection. Nothing broken or damaged!

I unlocked the door, sat behind the wheel, buckled up and turned the key in the ignition. I half expected the car not to start, but it fired first time. I checked the dials and could see I had plenty of petrol and the oil was fine, as was my cooling system. There was nothing to stop me. I manoeuvred the car onto the road and started driving in the direction of the church, my mind focused on what awaited me. All kinds of thoughts flickered and faded. Some of them were a bit silly, like people shouting hallelujah.

The church was in a predominantly Muslim area and on the way I passed the largest mosque in my city. As I did, the documentary came to my mind and I thought about how I could have almost been snared by the makers of that film series.

When I reached the road which the church was on, it was jam-packed. There was just a single file gap to drive down and as I did from one end to the other, looking for a space to park, I could see cars were parked bumper-to-bumper on both sides. It was so crammed; the road was very difficult to drive down. I believe there was a wedding taking place nearby and with people also turning up for the service at the church, plus the local residents, I suppose I shouldn't have been surprised.

At the bottom of the road there was a dead end, which meant the road I was driving on was the only way in or out. Fortunately, nothing was coming the other way so I drove slowly and carefully, hoping against hope to find a space to leave my car. As I made my way down, getting near the end, I passed the church on my left and looked at it. It was a small building and certainly nowhere as big as I'd been expecting, as I thought God's house would be quite an impressive size. Nevertheless, I was intrigued.

I was almost at the dead end and still hadn't found anywhere to park. It didn't look good. Without realising I had a quiet word with God, telling Him: *Lord, there doesn't appear to be any parking today and in addition with my poor health, I will instead come back another time when it isn't so busy and more convenient.* So I reached the end, manoeuvred around at the dead end and started on my way back up the road homeward bound. As I slowly passed the church, this time on my right, I casually glanced over and slammed on my brakes. Directly in front, there was now a space! Confused, I immediately looked up the road to see who had just left. The car space had definitely not been there seconds earlier. No one had left. The gap all the way up to the start of the road was empty, with just the same crammed up cars alongside. This was now the only space on the entire road. Today was the day that I had to go in. Still surprised, I thanked God and reveresed my car into the space. I sat for a moment and reflected that God must have heard me and performed a miracle. For a moment, I wondered if my future will now be filled with these kinds of amazing miracles or whether it was that God has to step in from time to time to just usher us a little so we are on track when seeking truth. I offered up a silent prayer of thanks, but didn't dwell on it, as I was keen to go in. Locking the car, I made my way over to the entrance.

I pushed open the door and found there was someone there to welcome me. We exchanged a few pleasantries before I walked through the hallway that led into the main church, where I could hear beautiful singing; people praising God through song. I was greeted warmly, and as I took a seat I looked around. I experienced a deep sense of satisfaction.

I'd made it! And to top it all off, not only was the church a predominantly African one, but the Pastor was Indian!

I can conclusively say that I have found the truth and I have never looked back!

EPILOGUE

Since I have become a Seventh-day Adventist I have been greatly blessed, and I have to thank God for the kindness and mercy that He has shown me. I am completely undeserved to have this truth in my life and even though my salvation is determined by my obedience, I am happy to have such an amazing advocate in Jesus Christ who will represent me on that great day of judgement that is before us all. I'm extremely thankful for the plan He had for me and by the manner in which He made things come together. Firstly, with Larissa, being a messianic Jew and not pushing "church" onto me had not only kept me away from the influence of church organisations early on but gave me time to contemplate on Jesus and Jesus alone. Secondly, with learning about the true-life story of Roger Morneau, deeper spiritual things became clearer to me. I have experienced unexplainable bizarre things in my life growing up so watching his amazing testimony not only gave me an full understanding of the battle between Christ and Satan but made me realise why things had happened in my life the way they did. For the first time, I was able to see the cunningness and lengths that Satan is prepared to go to in order to deceive humanity.

It is with regret to say that not everything has been as plain sailing as I was expecting it to be. I was expecting a perfect church that represents God in the highest order but as I mentioned earlier, I had not even heard of Seventh-day Adventists before. Jehovah's Witnesses (who have 8 million followers worldwide), I had heard of, but Seventh-day Adventists who have a global following of 25 million I had not.

Why are the church members in a state of sleep and not going forward with this incredible information they have? Well, the Bible is clear...

Revelation 12:17 says *"And the dragon was wroth with the woman, and went to make war with the remnant of her seed, which keep the commandments of God, and have the testimony of Jesus Christ."*

As we are on the cusp of receiving a mandatory Sunday law things are heating up. Satan knows his time is short and his objective is to take as many people down with him as possible. Along with this, the Bible reveals that the end-time church will be lukewarm in their actions and will be apathetic:

Revelation 3:16-22 *"So then because thou art lukewarm, and neither cold nor hot, I will spue thee out of my mouth. Because thou sayest, I am rich, and increased with goods, and have need of nothing; and knowest not that thou art wretched, and miserable, and poor, and blind, and naked: I counsel thee to buy of me gold tried in the fire, that thou mayest be rich; and white raiment, that thou mayest be clothed, and that the shame of thy nakedness do not appear; and anoint thine eyes with eyesalve, that thou mayest see. As many as I love, I rebuke and chasten: be zealous therefore, and repent. Behold, I stand at the door, and knock: if any man hear my voice, and open the door, I will come in to him, and will sup with him, and he with me. To him that overcometh will I grant to sit with me in my throne, even as I also overcame, and am set down with my Father in his throne. He that hath an ear, let him hear what the Spirit saith unto the churches."*

Regardless of the state of the people in this church, as we approach the end of Earth's existence, God has been merciful in allowing the name of Jesus to be spread around the whole world. Us humans are all in agreement as to who is the most popular figure in the history of this planet. To not make an enquiry is our own choice. We are not in the Dark Ages anymore where Bibles have been taken away from us. We are in a time where we have easy access to a wealth of information; information that can be assessed and logically processed. People who think that they will be able to turn to God and say "You never showed me" are actually kidding themselves. It's really more of a case of "I didn't want to know". And therefore not wanting to know has signed your future over.

Matthew 24:11- 14 *"And many false prophets shall rise, and shall deceive many. And because iniquity shall abound, the love of many shall wax cold. But he that shall endure unto the end, the same shall be saved. And this gospel of the kingdom shall be preached in all the world for a witness unto all nations; and then shall the end come."*

Another sorrowful experience I have had since becoming a Seventh-day Adventist has involved my family. Not with regards to support, on the contrary, they have been amazing. My parents have really allowed me to embrace this as they have seen the fruit of my conversion. No, sadly, my issue has been with their salvation. In the grand scheme of things this is a really important topic, in fact, the most important topic and I was really hoping that my Dad and Mum would have discussed and embraced this exciting truth, at the very least for the sake of a brighter future in the next life. Sadly, it hasn't been the case. Nor has it been the case with my siblings, who I thought would at least scrutinise what I have brought to the table, then they would see that this is obviously the truth. Unfortunately, it hasn't transpired that way. When you find the truth you are extremely excited and assume that everyone will explore your findings and gladly take them on board but I have learned that, as heart-breaking as it is, it doesn't quite go to plan like that. In my Dad and Mum's case, I suspect there is no real reason other than tradition and the power it has over their lives. They are quite old now and so to give up everything that they have ever known, I guess, is extremely hard for them, especially as they have a temple in their home. As for my siblings, they are living for this world and like the majority of the people on this planet, the focus is on short-term fulfilment and the ultimate future is left unexplored. I have been able to learn, that in reality, finding out truth is not for everyone and I have come to realise that the same spirit of wanting to know truth or to at least make an enquiry for it, which exists in me, does not necessarily exist in others.

However, as much as I love my father, mother, sister, brother and sister, I know that God loves each one of them even more than I do, so every single day that passes, my wife and I raise every one of them up in prayer with the hope that someday they would make the important enquiry.

Thankfully God has placed me in positions where I have been able to share the message and see the fruits of it, which has brought me great joy and confirmed that His people are out there, waiting. One particular time that comes to mind is when my wife and I were at the Sydney Harbour watching a fireworks show. At the end we decided to get something to eat, it's amazing how hard it still is to genuinely find healthy vegetarian food out and about. So after much searching, thankfully we came across a hotel which had a restaurant with a decent menu. As we went in we were a bit surprised that the place was empty and were hoping it wasn't a reflection of the food that they were serving. My wife grabbed us a table as I went to the bar person and ordered. At some point he struck up a conversation which was external to the order and it was off the back of my accent. While placing the details through the till we spoke and he told me he was an American and studying in his final year at university. I was able to share snippets of my life with him and somehow the questions he asked led me to talk very briefly about my past and of course my faith. Once the order was processed, I then went away and joined my wife at the table. After a little while, at some point he approached our table (when the manager had temporarily disappeared out of the restaurant) and the first thing he said to me was "Hey, can you school me please?" I was taken a back. Not being down with street slang anymore I was glad I was able to work out what he was asking me. He went on to tell me that he knew something was coming over this world, he could see it in people's attitudes generally but especially in nature and through the media, news and movies etc. My wife and I were able to talk to him in further detail and ended up giving him a copy of *The Great Controversy*.

God is continually showing His kindness by allowing each and every human being, the gift of a fresh opportunity every morning, to take time out in life to seek out what is true, but in Jesus' own words we see that "... *they received not the love of the truth, that they might be saved.*" (2 Thessalonians 2:10).

It's such a shame and quite strange that people in the world who have the capacity to enquire to know more in regards to spiritual things. Even just looking at how wonderful and vast the planet in which we live in is, makes one ponder on the who, why, when and where of how this place came into existence. This can be better said by one of my favourite authors E.G White:

"Many are the ways in which God is seeking to make Himself known to us and bring us into communion with Him. Nature speaks to our senses without ceasing. The open heart will be impressed with the love and glory of God as revealed through the works of His hands. The listening ear can hear and understand the communications of God through the things of nature. The green fields, the lofty trees, the buds and flowers, the passing cloud, the falling rain, the babbling brook, the glories of the heavens, speak to our hearts, and invite us to become acquainted with Him who made them all." (Steps to Christ p85)

I couldn't imagine anything scarier that going into a future abyss with nothing more than a supposed hope – it's insanity! If people are happy to sit down and gain knowledge on things that will be insignificant at the end of their lives why can they not enquire of truth? The world seems to be under a spell of some kind.

I have learned that there has to be a love for the truth, you must want it more than anything you have ever wanted and you must be prepared to put it first. The reason? **God is Truth**!

John 8:32 *"And ye shall know the truth, and the truth shall make you free."*

APPENDIX A
A NEAR FATAL STORY

None of the close shaves with death I have experienced in my life are any more worrying than another. I have decided to include the following story as it correlates with my visit to India which was mentioned early on in this book. As I had stated, when I was much younger, I was a very awkward child. I suffered with a bad temper and was often irritable for no apparent reason. I was also very rebellious and a bit of a tear-away. My behaviour was appalling and caused my parents and siblings a great deal of anguish, heartache and worry. As a last resort, my mother took me to India for a pilgrimage around the temples. The objective was to get me out of my environment for a while in the hope that I would calm down and start behaving in a more sociable and less obnoxious manner. Both my parents thought that through acts of prayer and committing lots of offerings to the gods, peace would be bestowed upon me. Sadly, it wasn't to be. As mentioned, changes did occur in my life though, but not in the way they were expecting. I did calm down in some aspects but that had nothing to do with the temples, prayer and offerings. Rather, it was due to seeing the unbelievable level of poverty, because that really touched a nerve and caused me to appreciate certain things in my life.

For the majority of our stay there, my mother

decided to base us at her uncle's farm, as he was the closest family member in that country. That was because my parents had been born and brought up in Uganda, Africa, during the reign of Idi Amin, and so her immediate family were either elsewhere in the world or had sadly passed away. The farm was situated in Porbandar, a coastal city in the state of Gujarat, which is not only the town my mother's ancestors come from, but also Mahatma Gandhi. In fact, while we were there, I was taken to his house. That was an incredible experience, as back then, visitors were allowed literally inside and I got to see his famous cotton knitting wheel machine. A real privilege.

Overall, I had a superb time in India, and I loved the farm. It's still one of the fondest memories of my life. But it wasn't all perfect, and we experienced a few things that we would rather not have. One of them was the poverty that I alluded to before. It was heartbreaking to see other human beings reduced to such a low level, especially the street kids. We have all read about such poverty and seen it on the TV news, but until you actually come face-to-face with it in the flesh, with hand on heart, I can honestly say that you haven't even skimmed the surface of the worst of it. When you're amongst it every day of your life, you can't just turn it off, as you would a TV, or fold it over, as you would a newspaper, and then banish it from your thoughts until next time. When you are there, in the heart of it, it wrenches at your guts and pulls on your heartstrings and other emotions with a force that is so primal, it literally shakes you to your core and makes you question the way in which this planet is being run and why it is so. At least, that's how I felt. What I experienced in India will go with me to my grave, and it's a constant daily reminder of how well off I am in all aspects of my life even if I do experience a few upsets and things not going to plan from time to time. Compared to the poverty I saw; those are miniscule.

Another thing which shook us up was an incident that took place on our second night of arriving. My mother's uncle's farmhouse was in three sections. From right to left, there was the farmhouse itself, a very humble building, then next to that, room A and then room B. Rooms A and B were extensions that had been added on some time after the building of the main house. They did not match the original build, but nonetheless they were perfectly fine. The only real difference was in terms of the interior. The beams were exposed and it was possible to see the underside of the roof. As my mother and I were visiting guests, we were allocated room B, in which we shared a bed. The rest of my mother's uncle's family split themselves between room A, the house and the actual courtyard. There were quite a lot of people, many who knew my mother's family, and in particular my mother's parents, who had travelled far and wide to visit us. Having journeyed such a long way, they decided to stay. While the women and children slept inside, all the men retired to the courtyard, in front of the house, where they slept on khatiyas. For those of you who don't know, a khatiya is an Indian bed made out of four wooden posts and woven rope. It's very lightweight, comfortable and surprisingly durable. I think the family must have borrowed some from the neighbours, as there were so many available.

My mother and I went to bed at about 10.00pm, while the rest of the women and children went to their allocated rooms and the men stayed up outside, chatting and catching up. Before very long, both my mother and I, still feeling the exhausting effects of our long flight and journey from the airport to the farm, fell asleep. We were dead to the world. Then a bit later, I was awoken by the sound of a massive dull thud at the end of the bed. I stirred as I rubbed my eyes, it was pitch black. My mother also woke up. At the same moment, there was a knock at the door. It was one of my uncles enquiring to check if we were okay. He'd been sleeping outside in the courtyard. One thing I realised about my uncles was that they have incredible hearing, living on a farm and having to be on alert and standby they can hear things for miles on end.

"Are you okay, sister?" he asked through the door.

"Yes, thank you," my mother replied.

"Are you both okay? What was the noise I just heard?"

"We're both fine" my mother replied. "It was probably one of the suitcases or something falling over I think."

"My sister, I would really like to come in to make sure if that's okay."

That last comment baffled my mother, but she said, "Yes, sure."

I was still in the process of fully waking up but

could hear the door open and saw the light of a candle come into the room. The next thing I remember was being aggressively grabbed by my mother and rushed out into the back of the courtyard. I looked on as more of my uncles went into our room with candles and torches. About five minutes had passed and I was wondering what was going on, then all of a sudden they slowly came back out carrying a really huge cobra!

The farm was predominantly producing peanuts and some storage sacks containing them had originally been kept in the room which we were staying in, as they'd had a large harvest. They can attract mice and mice in turn attract snakes. My uncles believed it must have made its way into that room looking for mice and at some point made its way up on top of the beams in the room. Eventually it must have lost its placing. It could have been fatal.

APPENDIX B
REVERSE ENGINEERING

Not long after my conversion I decided to revisit my previous faith and other faiths to find out if I would have been able to recognise the truth without divine intervention.

I already had a fairly decent knowledge of Hindusim as it was the faith we held in the household I grew up in and I'd always ask my mother for information when something was on my mind. At times when I wanted to know something more involved, I delved into the Vedas and the Gita for answers. Sometimes the answer I would receive would be fine and clear, for example, a great answer I received was when at one time I really wanted to know if I should be eating meat or not. Historically Hindus don't. Nowadays, other than the Hindu priests, a majority of the people I know have adapted their mind-sets to start eating it as they have embraced western attitudes. One caveat that was created was that only cow eating was frowned upon, as cows are sacred. Not one for following the masses, I just wanted the facts. A priest had told me that God loved all animals so I was left scratching my head as to why we are eating them then and elevating the cow only. I was conflicted for ages, but I knew that eating an animal involved something that makes me uneasy - killing! And that blood was not placed there for us to simply take it away, so I felt a conviction that I was not to eat it, especially as the priests who are technically looking to get themselves right in the sight of God, abstained from it, so why shouldn't I? Not to mention, the other major factor in my life, that my mother is a vegetarian. I wanted to do the right thing, so I went on a quest to find the answer. After a not too difficult search, I came across a small community of Hindus online that took their faith very seriously. From the way they conducted themselves and handled the sacred books, I was able to conclude that they are the best team of scholars that I have come across who study Indian scriptures thoroughly, with an intellectual approach, very logically placing emphasis on the Vedas first and foremost (as they are the foundation of Hinduism) and searching out and reasoning the other texts, which have been written later in history, if they had conflicting information. They presented the case regarding animal eating and after a simple study with them, I had closure - I must not eat animals. In fact the study actually ended more involved as they showed me that I must not drink alcohol either. It took some time to get my head around it but I couldn't believe that I, as well as the mass majority were being been so obtuse. Imagine going to a friends house and they have told you specifically to take your dirty shoes off before you enter their home, but you completely ignore their request and continue to enter repeatedly, thinking you're being a good friend to them. How long do we think they will remain friends with you?

However, as I got older my questioning

became more intricate and I just couldn't receive an intellectual answer. The complex questioning arose when I realised the elitism of Hinduism. The fact that you cannot ever become a Hindu unless you are born one was strange for me to accept. My thinking behind all this was something like…

"How does the third largest religious group in the world with its various factions, as well as multiple gods and goddesses, have the truth?" When researching the history of Hinduism, in addition to the fact that the answers to my questions were inadequate and just didn't make sense, it was this elitism that was the clinching factor in my decision to look further into other faiths.

One thing I didn't get closure on, and I was really disappointed, was when I looked for a conclusive answer about reincarnation. To believe in reincarnation requires a lot of faith. My disappointment with this particular enquiry was that believing in it makes the value of human beings go down, in the sense that the creator isn't willing to create anymore but just allow creations to leap into other bodies, depending on the good works that they have done, thus the acceptance of the various caste systems, some of which is very cruel and unfair. Another thought on reincarnation was that I didn't want to have random and innumerable fathers, mothers and siblings etc. The family that God has given me are special to me and especially for me. Thankfully my new faith gave me an answer to this.

With all other faiths besides my old one, I did the same. I looked at them historically, highlighted the things I didn't like or agree with and searched out the answers of those particular things. I also analysed testimonies (books and videos) of ex-members as to why they had left that particular belief system to get a grasp on the whole thing.

There are countless Seventh-day Adventists who have converted from other faiths, and who have analysed their previous belief systems and identified where they believe that belief system to fall short. There would be no point in me writing everything here that these people have previously investigated so I will include details of these resources at the end of the book for you (the reader) to study and prayerfully ask your own questions. What I have done is taken an impartial historical view of things. The following information which I've included as separate appendices will give you a better understanding as to why I believe that Seventh-day Adventism is the only religion fully aligned to the truth.

One of the main reasons is that they follow the Ten Commandments. For more details on this, see Appendix H.

Was Jesus Real?

Is the most popular man in history, real or is he a made up person from past fictitious stories?

The period in which Jesus lived was around 1-4BC to AD30-36 depending on when the historian you refer to believes dating first began. In that timeframe, he had interactions with numerous people who were not just Christians. His life has been recorded outside of the New Testament by some very important people, not only Christians but also Jewish, Greek and Roman historians.

Scholars agree that the abundant historical accounts along with the Bible accounts of Christ all prove that there is no denying that Jesus Christ is real!

Scholars outside the Bible provide non-Christian validation that Christ existed. One widely accepted is the writings of Tacitus, a Roman historian who wrote literature confirming that Jesus Christ lived and his crucifixion was a real event. Likewise, the Jewish historian Flavius Josephus refers to Jesus Christ in his writings as the Messiah who was a wise teacher and crucified by Pilate. Similarly, Pliny the Younger was the Roman governor of Bithynia (now known as Turkey), who wrote letters about persecuting Christians in his time and how he was baffled that Christ's followers sang hymns to Him. In addition, the Babylonian Talmud is believed to contain various references to Jesus as "Yeshu".

In Jesus' own words He says, "Search the scriptures".

John 5:39 *"Search the scriptures; for in them ye think ye have eternal life: and they are they which testify of me."*

I have read various religious books including the Bible and I have absolutely no doubt in my mind whatsoever that the bible is the inspired word of God. It is a supernatural book that contains the accurate historical record charting the beginning of Earth's existence to its expected end. Further evidence is given throughout this appendix.

Has the Bible been Manipulated?

Have you ever heard someone say that you cannot trust the Bible because it has been manipulated? In my time, I have had many Muslims and Jehovah's Witnesses say this to me, time and time again. Of course, modern simplified translations have to be approached with caution, hence why most people who genuinely like to study prefer to use the King James bible version. But when statements about not trusting the bible at all are made, a few things come to mind. Firstly, if the Bible is from God, can't the Almighty protect His own book? If important historical documents have been preserved throughout many generations by mere human beings, then wouldn't an Almighty God better preserve His holy book? There are four very important statements within the Bible that can help with the answer to this, as well as some external history:

If any Man Adds to the Bible…

Here the prophet makes a damning statement. If anyone adds to the Bible, then God will take some vengeful acts out upon them as stated in:

Revelation 22:18-19 *"For I testify unto every man that heareth the words of the prophecy of this book, If any man shall add unto these things, God shall add unto him the plagues that are written in this book: And if any man shall take away from the words of the book of this prophecy, God shall take away his part out of the book of life, and out of the holy city, and from the things which are written in this book."*

We are to Compare things to the Bible to Discern Truth from Error

Acts 5:29 *"Then Peter and the other apostles answered and said, We ought to obey God rather than men."*

Acts 17:11 *"These were more noble than those in Thessalonica, in that they received the word with all readiness of mind, and searched the scriptures daily, whether those things were so."*

1 Thessalonians 5:20-22 *"Despise not prophesyings. Prove all things; hold fast that which is good. Abstain from all appearance of evil."*

This God-given counsel sets the action on how we should be assessing things. The Bible contains everything that is needed. If someone comes along with new information on God, how to worship Him, about the plan of salvation, or anything else for that matter, then these texts clearly point out that we should search the Bible and find the answer in it for ourselves. This will tell us what God says on the matter. It may give us confirmation or steer us away from error and deception. Similarly, the Bible says in:

1 John 4:1 *"Beloved, believe not every spirit, but try the spirits whether they are of God: because many false prophets are gone out into the world."*

Also, in:

Revelation 2:2 *"I know thy works, and thy labour, and thy patience, and how thou canst not bear them which are evil: and thou hast tried them which say they are apostles, and are not, and hast found them liars"*

Evidence from the Dead Sea Scrolls

In the article, *'Why are the Dead Sea Scrolls So Important?'* by One For Israel, it really delves into the importance of this fantastic historical findings. Two Arab mountain boys were looking for their goats and instead stumbled across a most amazing discovery - in a cave near the Dead Sea they found part of the long-hidden and long-lost Dead Sea Scrolls! As a result, between the years 1947-1956, over a thousand ancient manuscripts, which comprised the Dead Sea Scrolls, were found in 11 different caves. The article informs us that the text had identical copies of most of the Old Testament, proving that the Bible hasn't changed, since these documents were written about a thousand years before the earliest translation of the Old Testament from the 4th century. The article specifically states that, *"The Bible we have today is the same text as the text from the first century BCE, besides small changes in the lettering and very few textual changes, which are a common phenomenon in every ancient manuscript. This high level of preservation of the texts proves that the Old Testament we have today is a very accurate copy of the original text of Old Testament. There has been... no embellishment, and no corruption, and there is <u>physical evidence</u> to demonstrate this fact in the Israel Museum."*

Satan doesn't want people to read the Bible. In the Middle Ages, the Bible was taken away from the common people in an attempt to make them go to their priests directly for the repentance and forgiveness of sins. Many biblical truths were hidden away and this is why that period of time was also known as the Dark Ages. In time, however, God started awakening people with a sincere desire for the truth, starting with Martin Luther a Catholic priest and Professor of theology who wasn't happy with the Roman Catholic Church's teaching on *indulgences*. The Roman Catholic Church believes that by indulgences (repeating a specific prayer, going on a religious pilgrimage or by performing good deeds etc.), one can purify themselves and reduce the punishment he/she has to endure from God due to their sins. However, through Bible study Luther came to believe, taught and protested that salvation and, as a result, eternal life, are not earned by these deeds but are freely given by God as a gift of God's grace through the believer's faith in Jesus Christ. This challenged the authority of the Pope by teaching that the Bible is the only source of divine knowledge given from God and opposed *sacerdotalism* (the power of Catholic priests alone to reconcile our sins) but instead making it known that all baptised Christians are a part of a holy priesthood.

The Bible states that light is progressive:

Romans 16:25-26 *"Now to him that is of power to stablish you according to my gospel, and the preaching of Jesus Christ, according to the revelation of the mystery, which was kept secret since the world began, But now is made manifest, and by the scriptures of the prophets, according to the commandment of the everlasting God, made known to all nations for the obedience of faith."*

John 16:12-14 *"I have yet many things to say unto you, but ye cannot bear them now.*
Howbeit when he, the Spirit of truth, is come, he will guide you into all truth: for he shall not speak of himself; but whatsoever he shall hear, that shall he speak: and he will shew you things to come."

Therefore, as time progressed and people found new Bible truths, they set up a new church. For example, once the biblical foundation of baptism by immersion was discovered, Baptists came into existence. The continuation of searching the scriptures for further truth should have taken place and for some it did, the torch was passed on while embracing new Bible truths, but sadly for some it didn't. This is why we have many various denominations.

So with all the denominations we have today, can you tell who is the end-time church of God's people? Well, the answer is obviously going to be found in the Bible. A group who clearly use the Bible as the foundation of their beliefs and have taken on the truths available to fully follow the teachings of Christ can be found by a thorough Bible study. To find out, the key distinguishing features of this movement can be found in:

Revelation 12:17 *"And the dragon was wroth with the woman, and went to make war with the remnant of her seed, which keep the commandments of God, and have the testimony of Jesus Christ."*

It's pretty straightforward as to what it says. Firstly, we have to establish what it means by a remnant? Well, if you had a piece of material and after many years there is only a small piece left then that is the remnant, i.e. the remainder. So the end-time group will be like the first people in behaviours and actions. Secondly, they keep the commandments of God. All of the Ten Commandments and not a couple or nine as the regular Christian world does.

Here is an excerpt from the *Catechism* which you will find fascinating:

Question: Have you any other way of proving the Church has power to institute festivals of precept?

Answer: Had she not such power, she could not have done that in which all modern religionists agree with her, she could not have substituted the observance of Sunday the 1st day of the week, for the observance of Saturday the 7th day, a change for which there is no Scriptural authority.
Rev. Stephen Keenan, A (Catholic) Doctrinal Catechism, P174 (1857)

APPENDIX C
LIFESTYLE IS TRUE RELIGION

In his book *The Blue Zones*, Dan Buettner researched communities around the world that had higher levels of 100-year-old residents. According to census data, just 55,000 Americans reach 100; that's just .02%. Buettner's goal was to discover the specific factors that these communities shared so that we could learn from them. After completing his research, Buettner revealed only five communities as official "Blue Zones": Ikaria, Greece; Okinawa, Japan; Sardinia, Italy; Nicoya Peninsula, Costa Rica; and Loma Linda, California.

Loma Linda, California is the one that stands out because it's their faith that has helped them to live healthier and longer. These people are Seventh-day Adventists. Looking after their body to be in optimal health is central to their faith, because the Bible says that your body has been given to you by God and therefore you should look after it. To do this, they get regular exercise, are vegetarian, don't drink or smoke, and surround themselves with like-minded friends who share their values and support positive habits.

Loma Linda University, owned and operated by the Seventh-day Adventist Church, has collected data from thousands of people over the years in the Adventist Health Studies. The results showed that a 30-year-old Adventist man is likely to live more than 7 years longer than the average Californian man. For women, it was a 4.4-year difference. The differences were even greater for vegetarian Adventists.

Buettner, mentions in his findings that Seventh-day Adventists have maintained their longevity better than the Okinawans due to western influences, which have caused them to eat less of their traditional healthy staple foods of seaweed, sweet potato and turmeric and instead eating more rice, milk and meat.

Now that you know these astonishing facts, what can you do to live longer?

- Eat plants. 90 to 95 percent of your daily food intake should be fruits, vegetables, grains and beans. This is evidenced in the original biblical diet given to the first humans created of grains, fruits, nuts, and vegetables, Genesis 1:29: *"And God said, Behold, I have given you every herb bearing seed, which is upon the face of all the earth, and every tree, in the which is the fruit of a tree yielding seed; to you it shall be for meat."* Adventists encourage a well-balanced diet including nuts, fruits, and legumes, low in sugar, salt, and refined grains.

- Eat an early, light dinner: "Eat breakfast like a king, lunch like a prince and dinner like a pauper," A light dinner early in the evening avoids flooding the body with calories during the inactive parts of the day. It promotes better sleep and a lower BMI.

- Don't snack! Our society has developed the habit of grazing all day by eating snacks and sweets whenever the urge arises. This means we are not giving our digestive systems adequate rest. Stick to set times for breakfast, lunch and dinner.

- Avoid too much dairy. Many Adventists practice a vegan diet, and many others consume animal by-products sparingly.

- Have a cup of beans per day — this includes tofu! Tofu is great because it includes high-quality protein and fibre. If you're buying canned beans, read the labels to ensure they're not packed with too much sodium, sugar and chemicals.

- Limit your sugar to 28 grams or less (seven teaspoons) daily. Or even better, instead use natural products like honey or dates etc. to sweeten your foods.

- Drink lots of water.

- Get regular, moderate exercise. Daily walks are a great way to get in low-intensity exercises and can be a fun time to socialise with friends.

- The Seventh-day Adventist Church encourages and provides opportunities for its members to volunteer. This also helps you stay active, find a sense of purpose, and stave off depression by focusing on helping others.

- Rest! Adventists keep the 24-hour Sabbath

from sunset Friday to sunset Saturday, when they worship and focus on God, family and fellowship. They don't work or think on the cares of this world during this time and step away from the stress of the week. After church, they often get outdoors in nature.

These principles of health can be summarised by using the acronym NEWSTART:
Nutrition
Exercise
Water
Sunlight
Temperance
Air
Rest
Trust in God

For detailed information and videos on each principle, go to the following website https://www.newstart.com/about/

The diet appointed man in the beginning did not include animal food. Not till after the flood, when every green thing on the earth had been destroyed, did man receive permission to eat flesh.

In choosing man's food in Eden, the Lord showed what was the best diet; in the choice made for Israel, He taught the same lesson...Through them He desired to bless and teach the world. He provided them with the food best adapted for this purpose, not flesh, but manna, "the bread of heaven." It was only because of their discontent and their murmurings for the fleshpots of Egypt that animal food was granted them, and this only for a short time. Its use brought disease and death to thousands...

By departing from the plan divinely appointed for their diet, the Israelites suffered great loss. They desired a flesh diet, and they reaped its results. They did not reach God's ideal of character or fulfill His purpose. The Lord "gave them their request, but sent leanness into their soul." They valued the earthly above the spiritual, and the sacred preeminence which was His purpose for them they did not attain. (White, E.G. The Ministry of Healing, 311, 312, 1905)

God gave our first parents the food he designed that the race should eat. It was contrary to his plan to have the life of any creature taken. There was to be no death in Eden. The fruit of the trees in the garden, was the food man's wants required. God gave man no permission to eat animal food until after the flood. Every thing had been destroyed upon which man could subsist, and therefore the Lord in their necessity gave Noah permission to eat of the clean animals which he had taken with him into the ark. But animal food was not the most healthy article of food for man.

The people who lived before the flood ate animal food, and gratified their lusts until their cup of iniquity was full, and God cleansed the earth of its moral pollution by a flood...

After the flood the people ate largely of animal food. God saw that the ways of man were corrupt, and that he was disposed to exalt himself proudly against his Creator, and to follow the inclinations of his own heart. And he permitted that long-lived race to eat animal food to shorten their sinful lives. Soon after the flood the race began to rapidly decrease in size, and in length of years. (White, E.G, Spiritual Gifts. Volume 4A, 120-121)

APPENDIX D
A STONE COLD STORY

My friend Anand and I were standing at the bar of a busy student pub waiting to order a drink, when out in the distance we spotted some friends of ours in a crowd making their way over to us. One of the group members was Tanner, a friend of mine from my hometown, who had just happened to have chosen the same university and course as me. We had reconnected in the opening weeks and had been meeting out on nights out etc. either organised or randomly. As I saw him approach I could see by his smile that he had something to tell to me. We made the usual greetings and he came and stood by us while his friends all chatted away. He didn't waste any time telling me that he had some really amazing news… about wrestling.

Due to boredom, my friends and I had at some point gotten interested again in WWF wrestling. Since the 90s when it had grown stale, they had remodeled the show and the storylines had become a lot more interesting and even though we knew the matches were staged, there was an appreciation of the exhibition and the athleticism of the entertainers. Even though we knew some people who were diehard into it, as I said earlier, my close friends and I were just into it as a time filler, so the news Tanner had to share about wrestling usually wouldn't have bowled me over, but this was different. I could just tell by his face that he had something really big to share with me. As I asked what it was, he emphasised how incredible this information is. My friend Anand and I listened on closely. We didn't need to press any further as he couldn't contain it. He asked us to reacquaint our minds with Caterina. And we did, he had introduced us to her a few months prior and not only had we seen her out on a couple of occasions but she had also been over to our place with Tanner. We could tell that they had become good friends although we thought at the time he may have been dating her in private. He proceeded to tell us how her dad owns a law firm in London and that he has a really interesting case on at this moment which is also incredibly strange. I was already intrigued as the news I was expecting was to do with a storyline involving one of the main characters, but here he was telling us that real news was taking place. I wondered as to what on earth Caterina's dad had going on that involved wrestling. Tanner certainly had me gripped; more so now that I knew it was a true story. I pressed him to tell us what it was all about, but frustratingly he wouldn't. He went on to say that Caterina was joining him later in a club, and if we were going there later on in the night, which we were, then she will tell us herself.

I'd known Tanner for many years. From college we had connected and been friends all throughout. Although not in each other's pockets, I saw him as a pretty standup guy, we had become genuine pals. As he was of Indian decent, we had connected on that level and also his soccer team was the rival of mine so there was plenty of banter along the way. Due to this history between us I had not only valued our friendship but trusted him completely.

We ordered some drinks and found somewhere to stand as we chatted away having a catch-up. General life was the main topic on our lips but it felt as though there was an elephant in the room now, one which I could not ignore, so I asked him to just tell us what the big news was. He raised a smile on his face, clearly in his mind he was wondering if we were thinking about his cliffhanger. He reconfirmed that I wouldn't believe him if he told me so I was just better off waiting for Caterina to fill me in. I looked at Anand waiting to see his take on the matter but he just looked back at me just as confused, so I decided to just leave it at that and wait for later.

After about an hour, Tanner left for the club with his friends. Before we would join them again, Anand and I decided to go to a little bar that was quite a walk away but worth it for the music alone, as we had a different taste to most of our house and course mates, so we rarely got the chance and decided to go for it. The question was brought up once more with us both intrigued as to what Tanner wanted to share. Even though he had done it all with a smile I knew it was something of depth, else why the secrecy.

Two hours must have passed and then we reluctantly left the bar knowing that it would be closing soon and headed to the club which would be open most of the night. As we got in we did the rounds and bumped into more friends of ours. As we stood there chatting away, enjoying some beverages, I noticed Tanner standing nearby. At some point of me talking to my friends, he must have seen us and came over with his group. As I turned around to properly acknowledge him, I also noticed Caterina standing next to him. I said Hi to her and asked her how she was and how her law degree was going. She told me that she was generally fine, stressed with the workload but happy to be out. As we exchanged further pleasantries, Tanner wasted no time by bringing up the secret wrestling news. He directly asked her to tell me what she had told him. Immediately, I could tell by her face that it was kind of a big deal. There was no real shock from her, because whatever it was she must have known Tanner would have asked her to tell me. But she just had the look of someone who had big news, so I braced myself. She asked me if I was familiar with WWF wrestling (currently known as WWE wrestling). I nodded.

She went on to tell me that a few weeks back a lady had come to her dad's law firm in London and was seeking representation. She had said that she was married to a very famous WWF wrestling superstar but wanted to divorce him and preferred to find lawyers in England, as she was English and was looking to relocate back with her two daughters. I listened on and found what she was telling me, not hugely interesting but I suppose there was an intrigue into who the famous wrestler was.

After Tanner had hung the carrot in the

previous bar, I had become a little impatient, wanting the chitchat done with and just wanted to hear who it was already. Divorces aren't uncommon and are a sad reality of life, to me it wasn't really mega news, besides it felt like the whole process of revealing who it was was taking far too long.

Tanner then didn't help as he interjected and tried to get me to guess who the famous wrestler was. I stood there for a moment wondering. I deliberately decided to give terrible answers hoping that these two would become frustrated quick and just tell me straight away. Tanner clearly wanted this to carry on throughout the night when he asked me to guess some more, I did, and this time tried a little harder but I just didn't know which wrestlers had English wives. Anand even had a couple of guesses. In the end, I got fed up and asked him directly who it was. He then turned to look at Caterina, I joined him in looking at her waiting for the answer. Her face was wryly smiling.

"Bav do you know a wrestler called Steve Austin?" As I watched her say that name I felt Tanner look at me from the wings, smiling and waiting for a reaction. Yes, I did know "Stone Cold" Steve Austin. He was the most famous wrestler at the time and is also considered to be one of the best wrestlers of all time. I often marveled at his fame, it was quite surprising really as he wasn't really one of the most skillful wrestlers, compared to many other famous people who shared a ring with him. Not only that but he was also noticeably nursing poor knees. His character's persona was one of a ruthless guy with an "I don't care" view to things and it worked really well within a period of wrestling aptly called *Attitude*. Although there were others with similar outlooks, remarkably the wrestling company had painted him up as the person to follow by giving him the best storylines and having him involved in the main events. As a result of this marketing, the crowds lapped it up as the people followed him.

Well, there it was, the shock news that I most definitely was not expecting. I was surprised that he had an English wife more than anything, I sure wasn't expecting it as I'd seen interviews given by him and he was a self-proclaimed redneck from Texas so for him to be married to someone from Blighty was a bit comical, not unbelievable of course, just humorous to me. As the disbelief of this megastar wrestler's soon to be ex-wife, potentially using a friend's dad's law firm quickly passed, I noticed them both standing there still looking at me. "That isn't the main thing", Tanner said. "Wait until you find out on what grounds the divorce is taking place". My attention went to Caterina again.

Now my rash thought process immediately prepared me by making me think on the fact that the wrestler is of course an actor. Sure in the ring the moves are dangerous, but they are planned and coordinated very well, along with the storyline accompanying each show, which involves the wrestler pretending to be something or do something that they wouldn't usually do in their normal life, like any other theatrics industry. Sadly, there's a saying that "life imitates art" and I think I've lost count at the amount of times when I have heard of an actor having to battle the strains of being in character for extended periods of time. As they are in this mode for so long, it starts creeping into their regular life. So I was sort of expecting Caterina to say that this wrestler had become like his character on the show. A foul-mouthed, beer swilling, rebel that uses the moniker "The Texan Rattlesnake" and also used the phrase/slogan "Austin 3:16". My interest peaked as I listened intently for her to confirm what I was expecting. But Caterina told me something else, something that really shocked me. She told me that the lady wants to divorce him because over the last couple of years, he has become a Satan worshipper and has gotten into Satanism in a big way! I felt Tanner staring at me, waiting for my response. I looked and saw Anand standing there with a shocked expression, for a moment I'd forgotten he was there. I eagerly waited for a punch-line or something to this bizarre joke, but it never came. In the moment, I thought about what she had just revealed. I knew Caterina and Tanner well enough to know that they had better things to do with their lives than to pull a stunt like this. The whole thing just made no sense. I tried to coax out the punch-line out of her by laughing and saying that this has to be some kind of joke. But she earnestly defended her information and declared it as true. She went on to say that she knows the whole thing sounds really weird but the wife went in to the office to discuss things with her dad and his partners and this was in the middle of it all.

But "why" I thought, *why on earth would a famous wrestler like this be interested in Satanism?* So I asked her, "Why? For what reason had he gotten into such a thing for?" Catarina asked me if I knew that the WWF – World Wrestling Federation were going through a legal dispute and name change at that time. Again I nodded.

Anand and my interest in WWF wrestling had come at a very unique time. The company was coming under huge pressure from the animal charity The World Wildlife Fund, also known as WWF who had been around a lot longer. The charity had allowed the wrestling company to use the acronym, but under specific guidelines that they were to only use it in a way which would not harm the animal charity. Sadly, there were lines crossed and as a result the charity was all over them with lawsuits. With the charity having such a rich heritage and associations with royalty, there was absolutely no way the owner of the wrestling federation would stand a chance, so they had to accept that they would have to re-brand going forward, so what they did was to launch a campaign called Get the "F out". The company had actually gone as far as to incorporate this whole switching campaign as a storyline in their shows involving the wrestlers.

Get the "F out" was a play on words to show that the company was removing the F from WWF and would eventually morph into WWE, Federation would become Entertainment.

The switch didn't happen overnight, it actually had been planned and had taken a couple of years to implement. WWF wrestling is a billion-dollar business and something that grand would need things putting into place.

Catarina told me that the wrestling company was on the verge of being sued for large sums of money and the whole thing could have a huge detriment on the business long-term. During the name change the biggest rival company would have taken over leaving the WWF/WWE in tatters. The wife had gone into the law firm and apparently very candidly said that she was convinced that her famous husband had committed some kind of satanic pact that involved the lawsuit, his career and the owner of the wrestling company. As a result, it had not only changed her husband's belief system but changed him as a person completely.

I tried to dismiss it, but it was hard when looking at her sincerity. At the time I didn't really believe in Jesus or Satan. I knew God existed and I had seen and experienced things in my life which were supernatural from both sides of the Great Controversy, but this was too involving and direct.

I remember us all chatting about it for a while, mainly shocked, but after a short time we let the whole conversation slide. We never really addressed it again that night. Anand and I did chat about it very loosely the following morning. I believe in our naivety we concluded that people with lots of money and fame will follow anything to get even more money and fame - even if it's false.

The only other time that I did bring the conversation up again was about 6 months later when I was with a group of guys who were really interested in wrestling. When I told them about this story I remember them being really bowled over by it. I distinctly remember it unsettling a couple of them as they watched it regularly and had seen something in the show over the course of time that paralleled with what I was telling them.

On reflection of this story, for this book, I conducted some research and found out something really quite fascinating.

About once a year the WWE (as it is now known) holds a Hall of Fame ceremony. A wrestler (or occasionally a storyline celebrity) from the bygone era is picked and credited with their contribution to the show. All the most famous wrestlers over time have been selected and in order to initiate them, usually another very famous wrestler is invited to present them with the accolade. Very rarely, if the wrestler is really famous, then a celebrity will be invited in to present the honour. For example, in 2005 Sylvester Stallone was invited to induct Hulk Hogan into the Hall of Fame. In 2007 William Shatner was invited for Jerry Lawler.

Whilst looking through the list of hall of fame inductees and the people who have inducted them, I noticed something very interesting. Since the Hall of fame began in 1993, the owner of the WWE has inducted only three people in all this time. Now for the owner of the company to induct you, you must be extremely important.

1994 - James Dudley. The First African American to run a major arena in the United States.

2009 – "Stone Cold" Steve Austin. Wrestler.

2013 - Donald Trump. For his contribution to a storyline (pre-presidential).

I have often thought about this wrestler story. Could it be true, that these kinds of things go on behind closed doors with rich and famous people? Or were my friends, Tanner and Caterina, somewhere out there, laughing, at mine and Anand's expense, at a very unfunny and random joke.

APPENDIX E
IN PLAIN SIGHT

Was my story about the wrestler a one off or a fable? Or unbeknownst to us are the celebrities that we idolise involved in some kind of Satanism? As Roger Morneau reveals in his candid interview '*A Trip into the Supernatural*', a famous Canadian musician told him that you cannot get ahead in this life without *something* working behind you, implying that without Satan and his demonic agencies, you cannot become rich and famous.

In 2005, in a very candid interview with 60 minutes, musician Bob Dylan was asked by the interviewer Ed Bradley why he was still making music and touring:

Dylan: "It goes back to that destiny thing. I made a bargain with it a long time ago, and I'm holding up my end."

Bradley: "What was your bargain?"

Dylan: "To get to where I am now."

Bradley: "Should I ask who you made the bargain with?"

Dylan: "The chief commander."

Bradley: "On this Earth?"

Dylan: "On this Earth and the world we can't see."

Likewise, 1980s musician Marc Almond, who had a hit song, which was interestingly named '*Tainted Love*', with his band Soft Cell, gave a very candid story in his autobiography similarly entitled '*Tainted Life*'. He stated that at some point he had picked up a copy of the "Satanic Bible" and had recognised many truths in it. Then fast forward into the future, where a friend of his who happened to be a minister within the church of Satan, invited him to be initiated, to which he self describes himself as not one to miss "a chance to be relegated to the bad book" and therefore "immediately said yes."

On the day of the ceremony, he especially hired a black limousine and went to the appointed place, a small grotto in some woods. After secret words were said to him in private, Almond goes on to say, "I was thrilled, actually half expecting lightning to strike me down, and every hair on my neck stood on end and sweat broke out on my top lip." He went on to say, "I didn't really feel that different – well, maybe just a little wickeder".

Another real-life example of a hit singer, making it known that he associates with Satan is when Freddy Mercury at a music concert, in between songs, says to an audience regarding a pair of gloves he was wearing: "Do you like my claws? They are real diamonds. It was a present from the Devil himself. You don't believe me? (Looks at the band and in disbelief says...) they don't believe me!"

With the conditioning we have received it is now normal to think that Satan is a red, trident-carrying, cloven-hoofed being. These ideas stem from imaginative novelists of old, such people as Dante, but in fact the Bible very clearly describes him to look the opposite.

Ezekiel 28:13 *"...Thou hast been in Eden the garden of God; every precious stone was thy covering, the sardius, topaz, and the diamond, the beryl, the onyx, and the jasper, the sapphire, the emerald, and the carbuncle, and gold: the workmanship of thy tabrets and of thy pipes was prepared in thee in the day that thou wast created."*

In 2011, Megadeth front-man and ex-Metallica lead guitarist, Dave Mustaine, appeared on ABC Primetime Nightline and gave this eye-opening insight into Lucifer, *"The greatest lie he's ever told was convincing people he doesn't exist. And you see people that think he's red and he's got a goatee and a pointy tail and stuff like that. He doesn't. He's very beautiful. He's an angel. Why would he look like some monster? He's capable of looking just like you. He could be in this room right now. We wouldn't know it... It's a very scary thought."*

Dave has sold millions of records with songs such as *The Conjuring* and *Black Friday* as some of his biggest sellers. He has spoken openly in the past about his involvement in black magic and placing hexes on people, plus going as far as saying that the lyrics on one of his hit tracks contains black magic and a lot of instructions for hexes are on it. But now he claims to be a born-again Christian. Although Dave may believe he is following Christ, he is actually being duped by Satan like the majority of the Christian world. Jesus clearly says to "search the scriptures" and had he done so, Dave would have given up his old life completely instead of continuing rock and roll and death metal music in the name of Jesus. When answering why he supports bands who promote darkness he states that "there's a little darkness in us all" so he has used this to justify his stance on continuing.

On the surface, it appears that only certain celebrities make tongue in cheek comments from time to time, such as the ones that are rough around the edges and are now old but what about the others who are younger, the ones from the current generation? Upon closer examination, you realise that there are hoards that are not only making comments in interviews but are embedding ideas in scripts and song lyrics etc. People who are both high up the fame ladder or down below are all serving the same god, which is mammon. It appears that you cannot get far in this life without having to sign up to it.

Nicky Minaj says: There is an entity living in her called Roman who makes her say things that she doesn't want to.

Kendrick Lamar: While being asked about his song entitled *Lucie*, he confirms that it is about his demon called Lucifer and it's the negative energy that speaks to him and influences his writing.

Katy Perry: Told Ruby Rose in an interview that she sold her soul to the devil. Looking at her music videos she seems to want to celebrate the fact that she did.

Kanye West: Has mentioned selling his soul many times. At one of his concerts he was heard singing, "I sold my soul to the devil, it was a crappy deal, all I got was a few toys and a happy meal".

But what about those people who are not conversing with Satan but with a different, "friendly" entity or a deceased loved one? Is that okay?

Contrary to the propaganda that is being pushed in music and movies, that our deceased loved ones are watching down on us, the Bible is crystal clear; it is an abomination to be communicating with spirits. It clearly states that the dead are asleep and are not haunting or visiting us to relay non-biblical answers to questions we may have. Ask yourself, why would God want departed people we love, to watch us struggle and suffer down here? Viewings of starvation, rape, murder etc it doesn't make sense at all. No the visitors are in fact, all fallen angels masquerading. It doesn't matter how they are dressed up.

Michael Jackson: Other than the obvious of him using his celebrity status to promote being *Bad* in his song as well as grabbing and gyrating his crotch, which is installing sexual behaviour into our subconscious minds, Michael Jackson was heavily involved in occult practices. One technique to communicate with spirits involves being in front of a mirror for extended periods of time. Michael Jackson candidly stated to Psychic News, in February 1987, that not only does he participate in this practice but the ghost of Liberace communicates with him through this channel. "I have a secret room, with a moving wall and mirrors. That's where I talk to Lee. His is the voice I hear in there. I feel his presence so very close to me." He goes on to say that Liberace "…is like my guardian angel. He's even given me permission to record his theme song". Michael, may not have realised it but the being that was in the mirror was not Lee Liberace.

Spirit communication isn't just limited to musicians. Denzel Washington, as Bob Dylan did, spoke to Ed Bradley for 60 Minutes and directly stated that he channelled spirits into his body for his movie role and without them he would not have been able to give such a powerful onscreen performance. Shirley MacLaine also confirmed to an entire audience at an award show ceremony that the actor Jack Nicholson channels spirits. Mr nice guy, Jim Carrey has openly admitted to the practice of staring excessively into the mirror. The documentary, Jim & Andy: The Great Beyond, highlights his journey of channelling the "spirit" of deceased comedian Andy Kaufman for the filming of a movie, and then being stuck with the spirit entity in his body, causing him to have meltdowns and breakdowns.

Another interesting conversation was between Rolling Stone magazine and Musician Carlos Santana in March 2000:

The article states: *"Metatron is an angel. Santana has been in regular contact with him since 1994. Carlos will sit here facing the wall, the candles lit. He has a yellow legal pad at one side, ready for the communications that will come. 'It's kind of like a fax machine,' he says."* "*…you meditate and you got the candles, you got the incense and you've been chanting, and all of a sudden you hear this voice: "Write this down".*

"He tells me more about Metatron. 'Metatron is the architect of physical life. Because of him, we can French-kiss, we can hug, we can get a hot dog, wiggle our toe.' He sees Metatron in his dreams and meditations. He looks a bit like Santa Claus "white beard, and kind of this jolly fellow.' Metatron, who has been mentioned in mystical disciplines through the ages, also appears as the eye inside the triangle."

"Metatron wants something from me, and I know exactly what it is…The people who listen to the music are connected to a higher form of themselves. That's why I get a lot of joy from this CD, because it's a personal invitation from me to people: Remember your divinity."

Should we be praising Metatron on this forsaken planet and celebrating him for the joys of French kissing and eating hotdogs? With *mind clearance* and *automatic writing* Satan and his fallen angels are able to possess individuals and then manipulate humanity by what we watch and what we listen to. As Carlos Santana does not read the

Bible for guidance, the entities, which should I add appear when he is in a self-induced state, come speaking all manner of things that are contrary to the Scriptures. God inspires His people and doesn't need us to behave like mediums so that spirits can control the pen we hold.

It's clear from the interview that Metatron has no real interest in Carlos Santana. His interest is in making people believe there is something divine in them and also reaching kids through music for the anti-God embedded information.

These confessions are just the tip of the iceberg. The list of celebrity confessions is absolutely massive and there would be no point in writing everything down here as it is just an Internet search away.

Why are these musicians singing about the Devil/Satan/Lucifer? Of all the things in the world to sing about, why that particular being? Is it just a bit of fun they're having? The truth is Satan wants glory, and through his agencies (celebrities) he will snare the public, but subtly. This is a game. Regardless of what someone professes to believe in, you can only get rich and famous if you make a deal with him, just like Satan tried to do when he met with Jesus as described in:

Matthew 4:8-10 *"Again, the devil taketh him up into an exceeding high mountain, and sheweth him all the kingdoms of the world, and the glory of them; And saith unto him, All these things will I give thee, if thou wilt fall down and worship me. Then saith Jesus unto him, Get thee hence, Satan: for it is written, Thou shalt worship the Lord thy God, and him only shalt thou serve."*

Why are the people whom we idolise professing Satan and also promoting other spirits? It's all confusion. A small examination into these celebrity's lives will reveal that they are working towards an agenda, which is to get people, especially their children to focus on self, which is the exact characteristic of Satan as described in Isaiah 14:12-14. Be it ones' image or even something like food, you name it and its plain to see: YOUtube, SELFies, MYspace etc. Uploading new items of clothing purchased or taking photos of a dessert, this will detach people from the realities of life and in the end, in times of peril they are left thinking and guessing and ultimately kept away from reading the Bible which gives the true plan of salvation. Through following others and with a relaxed approach, people will try (and are trying) to find connections to various belief systems. So instead of seeking the truth in an educated way, they try to bridge the gap and develop an attitude of *we are all one and the same*, and *there are many ways to reach God*, when in reality this is false, there is only one way and as you have read through the confessions of the world's rich and elite, they know it.

What this is leading up to is the **ecumenical movement** - a coming together of all world religions. On the surface all this appears good but in reality the Bible states that God doesn't change.

He has made the supreme sacrifice for us to be with Him and to try and find other methods or routes is completely disrespectful and is really just preparing the world for the <u>soon coming false christ.</u>

As we approach the end of time the assault has become so much more abundant. As I mentioned in my book *The Demons of Ayahuasca*, in Snoop Doggy Dogg's hit song *Murder was the Case*, the rapper clearly reveals how he got to where he is, by selling out to an entity. I have also seen interviews in which he confirms that he does believe in God. Sadly, the god which he believes in is not the same one that he will wish he had followed once this life is over. Like most of the other celebrities, when you look into their backgrounds they went through some kind of poverty or hardship which is why I believe they so readily gave up everything. These celebrities enjoy riches and fame for just a short while in exchange to dilute you, the unsuspecting follower. What was once holy and valuable in your life vanishes and all you have to show for it in this life is a selfish/rebellious nature and of course possessions that you will be leaving here.

As the end of the world draws near, Satan knows his time is extremely short so he is ramping up his efforts in order to hoodwink and take as many down with him as he possibly can.

Through the power of subliminal and subconscious messages, he implants anti-God ideas that are from him but the general public believe they are their own. Through music, movies, television, sports, the internet, advertising and so on, he has the masses connected. His agents (the actors/actresses/entertainers of this world) are willingly or unwillingly used to coax you, humankind at large, into a false sense of escapism, which thus leads to indoctrination and ultimately resulting in a rebellious and destructive lifestyle. Sometimes the "Kings of this world" are secretive about their satanic mission, whereas at other times they allow us a peek into their world, because either way the majority are deluded and none the wiser.

We need to think very logically about the aforementioned. If these multimillionaire superstars are following Satan then who is it that is on the other end of the spectrum? No global religious book that I have come across mentions Satan without mentioning Jesus. By studying these celebrities alone, it is a very simple to equate that Jesus is the truth.

*On writing this appendix, Actor Christian Bale was given a Golden Globe award for his acting. He got the internet talking, because midway through his speech he made a point to thank Satan for helping him with his role.

APPENDIX F
THE REAL AGENDA

Do the beliefs of these megastars impact what they relay to you and I? Is their "art" separate from their personal beliefs? Or do they and their masters have plans for you? People and mostly parents were extremely worried that The Beatles, Elvis and rock and roll music would generally be a detriment to society. Well, were they right? Here we are in 2019 and the world has become a mess while people make life about seeking fun and entertainment. The boundaries have been pushed and pushed and now we are in a place where a hate for God isn't such a secret agenda anymore.

One time whilst out in a shopping mall I heard a song come on the radio called *'I see fire'* which really unnerved me. The lyrics were that profound that I had to go home and search them to validate what I had heard. In it the singer Ed Sheeran was clearly talking about the biblical end of time but from his perspective, as he sat on the side of the lost. How many kids must be unknowingly singing along to that song indoctrinating themselves? It wasn't a one off. Around the same period on two separate occasions I heard two songs promoting similar agendas. The first was a song called *'Starboy'* by The Weeknd featuring Daft Punk. The lyrics talked about the singer wanting to try and hurt a "red lamb". If you are unsure as to who the red lamb in question is then by watching the music video and reading the lyrics through properly will no doubt convict you. The other, called *'Light it Up'* had similar end time preparation lyrics and even mentioned a wait for a messiah.

We know that music and entertainment such as movies has installed various habits into us. One example is that the world has become completely sexualised. So much so that it is an Achilles heel to some, in the sense that it frames their lives. Beats and lyrics to music, movie scenes, posters, fashion, semi naked photos on twitter or instagram accounts, people are walking around in a heightened sexual state of mind. But is the "god-mocking" to such an extent now that the usual conditioning of sex, self and rebellion now also being joined by another message that is basically preparing everyone for the acceptance of the impending doom? Well, if you genuinely look at what movies are being put out and are able to look deeper into the songs that we and our kids listen to (we have a habit of focusing on just the chorus) then we would be able to see things for what they are. Having phased listening to modern music out of my life, I am sure I have made the right choice and have gained benefits but unfortunately there are times when being in a public environment means you get to hear the garbage playing over the airways. In around this same period there was yet another song called *'Skyfall'* by a singer called Adele. The song was for a James Bond movie by the same name. Are these just random names for films and songs or something much more?

The deeper question is how many must have sung along to these songs? Is our repeat singing impacting us subconsciously? The words that these singers use and the structures of the songs are actually getting people ready to accept the doom that will be overcoming Ed Sheeran and his reprobate celebrity friends. They have made a choice and the price is to take **you** down with them, which they will gladly do out of their hatred of God by spoon-feeding you songs with hooks and repeat statements, hypnotically and unknowingly inducing you and your children.

APPENDIX G
HOLY WAR : THE GREAT CONTROVERSY

There is a spiritual war taking place which we are all a part of and it is very real. With all the aforementioned things, it is clear to see that we are on the cusp of things coming into play, which will happen in rapid succession.

1. A Cashless Society
Finances are being made electronic. Your transactions are being logged with your habits and your movements being analysed. They will be switched on and off as necessary, should you not heed to the powers that be. Whether you like it or not there are things taking place in the world that should make you sit up and pay attention.

Revelation 13:17 *"And that no man might buy or sell, save he that had the mark, or the name of the beast, or the number of his name."*

In India, almost overnight money has been made electronic. In the guise of protection, biodata of every single person has been taken. If the populated countries as well as the ones with severe poverty can be prepped, then countries in the west such as England, America and Australia will easily be changed.

2. National Sunday Law

There is a worldwide movement taking place that is looking to enforce Sunday, which means no worshipping of God on the biblical Sabbath. It is going to happen whether we like it or not. The problem with it is that it is against God's teaching as it is the only one of the ten commandments that points to God as the creator.

Exodus 20:8-11 "Remember the sabbath day, to keep it holy. Six days shalt thou labour, and do all thy work: But the seventh day is the sabbath of the Lord thy God: in it thou shalt not do any work, thou, nor thy son, nor thy daughter, thy manservant, nor thy maidservant, nor thy cattle, nor thy stranger that is within thy gates: For in six days the Lord made heaven and earth, the sea, and all that in them is, and rested the seventh day: wherefore the Lord blessed the sabbath day, and hallowed it."

As a result, those who wish to follow God will be facing a backlash if they have not fully prepared and accepted the counsels from the Bible and Spirit of Prophecy.

Oprah Winfrey recently released a book entitled, *'The Wisdom of Sundays'*. This is a very interesting title especially from somebody who promotes general spirituality as opposed to Christianity. Nicole Kidman also called her child Sunday.

3. Baba's Coming

My mother is friends with a lady who is associated with a sect within Hinduism. This sect, is interested in eating and living pure. They even generally wear white clothing.

One time, after a lengthy conversation with this woman, my mother returned home and she and I opened up dialogue. She proceeded to tell me that her friend had said that *Baba* was coming onto the world scene, very soon. At the time I had not long started at college so was relatively young and a little shocked by the statement. I believe my thinking at the time was rattled by the fact that I wasn't ready to meet my God.

Who is Baba that is coming soon? These people do not believe in Christ so they don't fully understand who it is, but we live in a world where statements such as "I'll believe it when I see it" or "seeing is believing" are common ground.

Isaiah 14:12-14 *"How art thou fallen from heaven, O Lucifer, son of the morning! how art thou cut down to the ground, which didst weaken the nations! For thou hast said in thine heart, I will ascend into heaven, I will exalt my throne above the stars of God: I will sit also upon the mount of the congregation, in the sides of the north: I will ascend above the heights of the clouds; I will be like the most High."*

It is clearly stated by Lucifer that he wants to be *like* the most high. It's a misconception that he is looking to be different. His dream has always been to be Christ himself and to take His throne. As Satan appeared to Jesus as an angel of light, so also in like manner will he be appearing again, soon, on the world scene impersonating God.

4. The State of the Dead

- In an interview with UK's *Mail on Sunday*, actress Naomi Watts said she was visited by the ghost of Princess Diana who gave her blessing for Naomi to act as Diana in a movie on her life. Simone Simmons, who was Princess Diana's closest confidant, also says she speaks to the princess regularly, with recent conversations being about voting for Brexit and how she is happy with Prince William's choice in marrying Kate!

- Singer Miley Cyrus disclosed in an *Elle UK* interview that both her and her sister saw the ghost of a little boy in the bathroom of her London flat.

- Star Wars actress Carrie Fisher claimed that her house was haunted by deceased Republican Strategist R Gregory Stevens.

- Singer Cher believes that the ghost of her ex-husband, Sonny visits her house.

- La Toya Jackson spoke with the ghost of her dead brother, Michael Jackson, by using a medium named Tyler Henry which aired on his show called *Hollywood Medium*.

- In an article published by *Daily Star*, it is reported that Lady Gaga openly claimed that she was being haunted by a ghost named, Ryan. She said he was "stalking" her at her concerts all over the world and it was becoming too much, so she hired a medium to help conduct a séance in the hope that he would leave her alone. Lady Gaga believed that he was a bad omen she received as she has had other dealings with paranormal spirits.

- Celebrity singer, songwriter, rapper and actress, Kesha candidly recaps in an interview with *Rolling Stone* the experiences she has with dead entities clinging to her and haunting her inside her body. It reached its peak when objects started flying off the shelves, so she called her healer (who she regularly visits) to get an exorcism. Kesha even reveals that during the exorcism, the healer spoke in tongues and was choking, ultimately succeeding with the spirits leaving her. It's quite interesting then that she has a song entitled, *Supernatural,* which talks about her personal sexual experiences with a ghost.

- Some of you might even find it hard to believe that there are numerous reports that the USA's longest serving First Lady Hillary Clinton communicated with the spirit of Eleanor Roosevelt.

So, were all these cognitively rational, influential people really visited by the ghosts of the deceased? We need to ask some really straight forward questions. Why on earth would God want Diana to communicate with an actress so that she (and her Hollywood friends) can make movies about her life? In fact, why would God want Cher to be visited by the ghost of her ex-husband or Eleanor Roosevelt to speak with Hilary Clinton?

The internet has made the world a small place, and as a result, we are seeing and hearing that more and more people all over the globe are being visited by ghosts, be it celebrities or non-celebrities. These experiences are becoming very common. Could it be that rational-minded people are collectively becoming confused or is there something behind these visitations? From deceased family members and historical figures to celebrities, it seems like everyone who passes away is quick in trying to come back and make contact with us. All this is being assisted/promoted by movies (such as *Ghost*) and various TV shows with mediums trying to make contact with the other side, even children's programs, such as *Casper the Friendly Ghost,* has been geared up for your kids to embrace communicating with spirits. Where are the dead once they die? Are they floating around, trapped in haunted houses or visiting us to comfort us, or is there a serious deception taking place that is preparing us for the soon coming revealing of Satan impersonating Jesus? The Bible says in Ecclesiastes 9:5-6 " *For the living know that they shall die: but the dead know not any thing, neither have they any more a reward; for the memory of them is forgotten. Also their love, and their hatred, and their envy, is now perished; neither have they any more a portion for ever in any thing that is done under the sun."*

Death is temporary unconsciousness, referred to in the Bible as sleep, which the dead person is in until the resurrection. To counteract this truth, Satan deceives people by lies and uses spiritualism to do so. Back in Eden with the first humans, Satan deceived Eve by telling her that she will not surely die. Nowadays he uses manifestations of the dead to trick people into believing his lies. These spirits are actually evil fallen angels who follow Satan and work with him to try to entice humankind into disobeying God. They can manifest into many things but often take on the appearance of dead people, usually someone who we admire, but we should be firm in our understanding that the dead are still in their graves. God knew Satan would do this and therefore has forbidden us to communicate with spirits. Leviticus 19:31 says, *"Regard not them that have familiar spirits, neither seek after wizards, to be defiled by them: I am the LORD your God."*

As a result of all of this deception, people are being hoodwinked into thinking that the dead are still alive and communicating with the living. Therefore, they don't see the importance of understanding the truth about death and their future judgement and resurrection, which can only be learned about in the Bible. Satan is diminishing intellect and placing our focus on this temporary life that will inevitably come to an end. A time is coming very soon when these visitations will be even more frequent and unfortunately, as people already have a "seeing is believing" attitude, they will easily be caught up in the mass deception.

5. Climate Change

Climate change has been highly publicised in the news as being of prime concern in recent years, so much so that it has become common knowledge worldwide. Not only does everyone know what it is but many have developed strong feelings associated with it. Large climate change protests, by adults and children alike, have taken place worldwide throughout 2019, with the most vocal including Austria, Australia, Belgium, Canada, Chile, England, Finland, France, Germany, Hong Kong, India, Portugal, South Africa, South Korea, Turkey, Ukraine and the USA. These protests were not only attended by thousands but included many arrests, student strikes, civil disobedience and displays that were life threatening, such as holding up signs on the roof of moving trains in London.

The World Council of Churches has been meeting at the Vatican to address the matter, where the role of religious leaders in encouraging "climate justice" has been promoted by people in high up positions, including the Secretary General of the United Nations. Along with the Pope, World Council of Churches General Secretary Rev. Dr. Olav Rykse Tveit in the following statement is appealing to Christians and the general public to be committed to global laws to stop climate change, *"[Churches in the past] did not question the unsustainable development path of industrialized societies with the reckless consumption of natural resources and the ever growing use of fossil fuels. We have to acknowledge these sins of the past in order to be credible today…We have called for actions, for a just and binding treaty among the nations to commit the nations of the world to change"*. Fast forward to November, 2018 where a climate change summit concluded with church leaders from across the globe all signing a petition to take urgent action to commit to address and limit the consequences of climate change.

Rabbi Yonatan Neril, the Director of the Interfaith Centre for Sustainable Development goes as far as to state that, "We can only address climate change by religious figures taking a leading role in helping to reorient humanity toward sustainable lifestyles."

No matter what the United Nations or world politics do to try and resolve "climate change" they will not be able to fix things to what they used to be. Even with a multitude of laws to protect nature, human effort is highly restricted. More importantly, it will not change the course of the consequence of rejecting the laws of God, but could this be what instigates the fulfilment of Satan's aims to ultimately blame God's people for upcoming catastrophic natural disasters?

The Pope, in 2015 called upon Christians and all people all over the world to take serious action to protect nature. Through this seemingly caring act, this action is leading the world to reject God's law and as a result increasing the withdrawal of God's blessings and protection. Satan will be given the go-ahead to greatly increase the carnage caused by the destruction of nature and the majority of mankind will say that it is God's judgments that are being poured out. They will point fingers at God's people who keep His law, specifically His seventh-day Sabbath, as the cause of God's displeasure.

His new encyclical, *Laudato Si'* is a candid

document in which he criticises rich countries for abusing the environment and blames bankers and climate sceptics for accelerating its decline. He warns of crop failure, economic ruin, mass migration and the destruction of entire eco-systems saying, "If the current trend continues this century we could witness climate change unlike anything seen before and the unprecedented destruction of eco-systems, with serious consequences for all of us." There is some truth to what he's saying, the Bible actually tells us that these types of things will happen. God warns us to get ready for the end times because we can't stop the decline of nature, which is a consequence of sin and already foretold in Bible prophecy.

This debate is putting pressure and guilt upon the human race so that the majority want to halt climate change and motivate political leaders to unite on having global environmental protection.

This lines up with Revelation 13 which tells us that a worldwide religion will form so that all who live upon the earth will worship the beast or his image. The joining of church and state is Satan's doing so that he can isolate God's people and leave them in a position where they will have to make a choice between following God's law or following man's law. *"…all the world wondered after the beast"* Revelation 13:3

Since the creation of the Earth and the Sabbath are linked, the Pope can use the concept of protecting creation with the protection of the papal sabbath, which popes have always assigned to Sunday, and this can lead humankind to accept a universal worship law aimed at reverencing Sunday over Sabbath and having a devastating impact on those who keep his true Sabbath (Friday sunset to Saturday sunset) found in the Bible, because they will be prohibited by law to do so.

Let us continue to keep our eyes on what is taking place in the climate change arena, where I believe that the Pope will continue to bring to the open other aspects of social concern, such as the environment, to bring Protestants and other religions closer to Rome as they unite together in protecting the environment and at some point may use it to enforce Sunday as a day of rest.

APPENDIX H
OPEN SECRET

Someone who wasn't really into studying their bible but had regular church attendance, once brought this bible text to a conversation that was taking place - they were initially very confident with their finding:

Colossians 2:16-17 " *Let no man therefore judge you in meat, or in drink, or in respect of an holyday, or of the new moon, or of the sabbath days: Which are a shadow of things to come; but the body is of Christ."*

Could this text be talking about the actual Sabbath of the ten commandments, that God wrote in stone with his own finger? Or could it be referring to the ceremonial Jewish laws which at the time were collectively called sabbaths, that pointed to the coming of the Messiah?

Looking at it carefully, its pretty obvious but in case there was any doubt, let us really consider each sentence of what is being said in the following quote:

"Perhaps the boldest thing, the most revolutionary change the Church ever did, happened in the first century. The holy day, the Sabbath, was changed from Saturday to Sunday. 'The day of the Lord' was chosen, not from any direction noted in the Scriptures, but from the (Catholic) Church's sense of its own power...People who think that the Scriptures should be the sole authority, should logically become 7th Day Adventists, and keep Saturday holy." St. Catherine Church Sentinel,

Algonac, Michigan, May 21, 1995.

The book "Rome's Challenge", is a very interesting compilation of articles written over the years in the *Catholic Mirror*. In it is a collection of many articles which really challenge the protestant Christian to think about why they are keeping Sunday holy, when non Protestants (the Roman Catholics) changed the biblical day of worship from Saturday to Sunday. Are protestants not protesting anymore? The book really should be embarrassing to Christians, who are not Catholic, that defend keeping Sunday holy as it exposes their lack of bible study, especially in light of Daniel 7:25 which clearly talks about the changing of times and laws.

The following statements are a few of many that have been released over the years, from some very studious people and Christian organisations, that confirms the true position and history of the Sabbath.

<u>Roman Catholicism</u>
No such Law in the Bible

Question: Which is the Sabbath day?
Answer: Saturday is the Sabbath day.
Question: Why do we observe Sunday instead of Saturday?
Answer: We observe Sunday instead of Saturday because the Catholic Church transferred the solemnity from Saturday to Sunday.

Rev. Peter Geierman C.SS.R., *The Convert's Catechism of Catholic Doctrine*, P50 (1957)

But you may read the Bible from Genesis to Revelation, and you will not find a single line authorizing the sanctification of Sunday. The Scriptures enforce the religious observance of Saturday, a day which we never sanctify.

Cardinal James Gibbons, *The Faith of Our Fathers*, p89 (Ayers Publishing, 1978)

If Protestants would follow the Bible, they should worship God on the Sabbath day. In keeping the Sunday, they are following a law of the Catholic Church.

Cardinal Albert Smith, Chancellor of the Archdiocese of Baltimore (letter dated February 10, 1920)

Question: Have you any other way of proving the Church has power to institute festivals of precept?

Answer: Had she not such power, she could not have done that in which all modern religionists agree with her, she could not have substituted the observance of Sunday the 1st day of the week, for the observance of Saturday the 7th day, a change for which there is no Scriptural authority.

Rev. Stephen Keenan, *A (Catholic) Doctrinal Catechism*, P174 (1857)

Practically everything Protestants regard as essential or important they have received from the Catholic Church... The Protestant mind does not seem to realize that in accepting the Bible and observing the Sunday, in keeping Christmas and Easter, they are accepting the authority of the spokesman for the church, the Pope.

Our Sunday Visitor (February 5, 1950)

The observance of Sunday by the Protestants is a homage they pay, in spite of themselves, to the authority of the (Catholic) Church.

Louis Gaston Segur, *Plain Talk about the Protestantism of To-Day* (London: Thomas Richardson and Son, 1874)

The Catholic Church, for over one thousand years before the existence of a Protestant, by virtue of her divine mission, changed the day from Saturday to Sunday.

The Adventists are the only body of Christians with the Bible as their teacher, who can find no warrant in its pages for the change of day from the seventh to the first. Hence their appellation, "Seventh-day Adventists."

The Catholic Mirror (September 23, 1893)

It was the holy Catholic Church that changed the day of rest from Saturday to Sunday, the 1st day of the week. And it not only compelled all to keep Sunday, but at the Council of Laodicea, AD 364, anathematized those who kept the Sabbath and urged all persons to labour on the 7th day under penalty of anathema.

Catholic Priest T. Enright, CSSR, Kansas City, MO

I have repeatedly offered $1000 to any one who can furnish any proof from the Bible that Sunday is the day we are bound to keep...The Bible says, "Remember the Sabbath day to keep it holy," but the Catholic Church says, "No, keep the first day of the week," and the whole world bows in obedience.

Catholic Priest T. Enright, CSSR, lecture at Hartford, KS (February 18, 1884)

The [Catholic] Church is above the Bible, and this transference of the Sabbath observance is proof of that fact.

Catholic Record (September 1, 1923)

Of course the Catholic Church claims that the change was her act...And the act is a MARK of her ecclesiastical power and authority in religious matters.

Letter from C.F. Thomas, Chancellor of Cardinal Gibbons (October 28, 1895)

Not the Creator of the Universe in Genesis 2:1-3, but the Catholic Church "can claim the honour of having granted man a pause to his work every seven days."

S.C. Mosna, *Storia della Domenica*, P366-367 (1969)

The (Catholic) Church changed the observance of the Sabbath to Sunday by right of the divine, infallible authority given to her by her Founder, Jesus Christ. The Protestant claiming the Bible to be the only guide of faith, has no warrant for observing Sunday. In this matter, the Seventh-day Adventist is the only consistent Protestant.

The Question Box, The Catholic Universe Bulletin (August 14, 1942)

You may not be aware of it, but there is a strong push being made within countries worldwide to implement a National Sunday Law. What you may be little more familiar with is the fact that nations are slowly embracing a cashless society. Both will work in tandem to enforce the Mark of the Beast.

American Congregationalists
No Authority in the New Testament for Substitution of the First Day for the Seventh

"The current notion that Christ and His apostles authoritatively substituted the first day for the seventh, is absolutely without any authority in the New Testament." Dr. Lyman Abbott, in the Christian Union, June 26, 1890

Anglican
Nowhere Commanded to Keep the First Day

"And where are we told in the Scriptures that we are to keep the first day at all? We are commanded to keep the seventh; but we are nowhere commanded to keep the first day. The reason why we keep the first of the week holy instead of the seventh is for the same reason that we observe many other things, – not because the Bible, but because the church, has enjoined [commanded] it." Isaac Williams, *Plain Sermons on the Catechism*, Vol. 1, pp 334, 336.

Anglican/Episcopal
The Catholics Changed it
"We have made the change from the seventh day to the first day, from Saturday to Sunday, on the authority of the one holy, Catholic, Apostolic Church of Christ." Episcopalian Bishop Symour, *Why we keep Sunday*.

Baptist
Sunday Sabbath Not in The Scriptures
"There was and is a commandment to keep holy the Sabbath day, but that Sabbath day was not on Sunday. It will be said, however, and with some show of truimph, that the Sabbath was transferred from the Seventh to the First day of the week, with all its duties, privileges and sanctions. Earnestly desiring information on this subject, which I have studied for many years, I ask, where can the record of such a transaction be found? Not in the New Testament – absolutely not. There is no scriptural evidence of the change of the Sabbath institution from the Seventh to the First day of the week...

"I wish to say that this Sabbath question, in this aspect of it, is the gravest and most perplexing question connected with Christian institutions which at present claims attention from Christian people; and the only reason that it is not a more disturbing element in Christian thought and in religious discussion is because the Christian world has settled down content on the conviction that some how a transference has taken place at the beginning of Christian history.

"To me it seems unaccountable that Jesus, during three years' discussion with His disciples, often conversing with them upon the Sabbath question, discussing it in some of its various aspects, freeing it from its false glosses [of Jewish traditions], never alluded to any transference of the day; also, that during forty days of His resurrection life, no such thing was intimated. Nor, so far as we know, did the Spirit, which was given to bring to their remembrance all things whatsoever that He had said unto them, deal with this question. Nor yet did the inspired apostles, in preaching the gospel, founding churches, counselling and instruction those founded, discuss or approach the subject.

"Of course, I quite well know that Sunday did come into use in early Christian history as a religious day, as we learn from the Christian Fathers and other sources. But what a pity that it comes branded with the mark of paganism, and christened with the name of a sun god, when adopted and sanctioned by the papal apostasy, and bequeathed as a sacred legacy to protestantism!" Dr. Edward Hiscox, author of The Baptist Manual. From a photostatic copy of a notarized statement by Dr. Hiscox.

"There was never any formal or authoritative change from the Jewish seventh day Sabbath to the Christian first day observance" William Owen Carver, *The Lord's Day in One Day* p.49

Church of England
No Warrant from Scripture for the Change of the Sabbath from Saturday to Sunday

"Neither did he (Jesus), or his disciples, ordain

another Sabbath in the place of this, as if they had intended only to shift the day; and to transfer this honor to some other time. Their doctrine and their practise are directly contrary, to so new a fancy. It is true, that in some tract of time, the Church in honor of his resurrection, did set apart that day on the which he rose, to holy exercises: but this upon their own authority, and without warrant from above, that we can hear of; more than the general warrant which God gave his Church, that all things in it be done decently, and in comely order." Dr. Peter Heylyn of the Church of England, quoted in *History of the Sabbath*, Pt 2, Ch.2, p7

Congregationalist
The Christian Sabbath [Sunday] isn't in the Scriptures

"The Christian Sabbath' [Sunday] is not in the Scripture, and was not by the primitive [early Christian] church called the Sabbath." Timothy Dwight, Theology, sermon 107, 1818 ed., Vol. IV, p49 [Dwight (1752-1817].

Disciples of Christ
It is all Old Wives' Fable to talk of the 'Change of the Sabbath'

"If it [the Ten Commandments] yet exist, let us observe it… And if it does not exist, let us abandon a mock observance of another day for it. 'But,' say some, 'it was changed from the seventh to the first day.' Where? when? and by whom? – No, it never was changed, nor could it be, unless creation was to be gone through again: for the reason assigned [in Genesis 2:1-3] must be changed before the observance or respect to the reason, can be changed. It is all old wives' fables to talk of the 'change of the sabbath' from the seventh to the first day. If it be changed, it was that august personage changed it who changes times and laws ex officio, - I think his name is "Doctor Antichrist.""" Alexander Campbell, *The Christian Baptist*, February 2, 1824, vol 1, no. 7

Episcopal
Bible Commandment says the Seventh-day is Sabbath

"The Bible commandment says on the seventh-day thou shalt rest. That is Saturday. Nowhere in the Bible is it laid down that worship should be done on Sunday." Phillip Carrington, quoted in Toronto Daily Star, Oct 26, 1949 [Carrington (1892-), Anglican archbishop of Quebec, spoke the above in a message on this subject delivered to a packed assembly of clergymen. It was widely reported at the time in the news media].

Lutheran

"But they err in teaching that Sunday has taken the place of the Old Testament Sabbath and therefore must be kept as the seventh day had to be kept by the children of Israel...These churches err in their teaching, for scripture has in no way ordained the first day of the week in place of the Sabbath. There is simply no law in the New Testament to that effect" John Theodore Mueller, *Sabbath or Sunday*, pp.15, 16

"We have seen how gradually the impression of the Jewish Sabbath faded from the mind of the Christian church, and how completely the newer thought underlying the observance of the first day took possession of the church. We have seen that the Christian of the first three centuries never confused one with the other, but for a time celebrated both." *The Sunday Problem*, a study book by the Lutheran Church (1923) p.36

"They [Roman Catholics] refer to the Sabbath Day, as having been changed into the Lord's Day, contrary to the Decalogue, as it seems. Neither is there any example whereof they make more than concerning the changing of the Sabbath Day. Great, say they, is the power of the Church, since it has dispensed with one of the Ten Commandments!" Augsburg Confession of Faith, p.28; written by Melanchthon and approved by Martin Luther, 1530; as published in *The Book of Concord of the Evangelical Lutheran Church*, Henry Jacobs, editor (1911), p.63

Methodist
Jesus did not Abolish the Moral Law – No Command to Keep Holy the First Day

"The moral law contained in the Ten Commandments, and enforced by the prophets, He, Jesus did not take away. It was not the design of His coming to revoke any part of this. This is a law which can never be broken…Every part of this law must remain in force upon all mankind and in all ages; as not depending either on time or place, or any other circumstances liable to change, but on the nature of man, and their unchangeable relation to each other." John Wesley, *Sermons on Several Occasions*, Vol.1, No. 25

"It is true that there is no positive command for infant baptism. Nor is there any for keeping holy the first day of the week. Many believe that Christ changed the Sabbath. But, from His own words, we see that He came for no such purpose. Those who believe that Jesus changed the Sabbath base it only on a supposition." Amos Binney, *Theological Compendium,* 1902 edition, pp 180-181, 171 [Binney (1802-1878), Methodist Minister and presiding Elder.

Moody Bible Institute

"I honestly believe that this commandment [the Sabbath commandment] is just as binding today as it ever was. I have talked with men who have said that it has been abrogated [abolished], but they have never been able to point to any place in the Bible where God repealed it. When Christ was on earth, He did nothing to set it aside; He freed it from the traces under which the scribes and Pharisees had put it, and gave it its true place. 'The Sabbath was made for man, not man for the Sabbath' [mark 2:27]. It is just as practicable and as necessary for men today as it ever was – in fact, more than ever, because we live in such an intense age.

"The [Seventh-day] Sabbath was binding in Eden, and it has been in force ever since. This Fourth Commandment [Exodus 20:8-11] begins with the word 'remember,' showing that the

Sabbath had already existed when God wrote the law on the tables of stone at Sinai. How can men claim that this one commandment has been done away with when they admit that the other nine are still binding? Dwight.L. Moody, *Weighed and Wanting*, 1898, pp.46-47.

"This Fourth is not a commandment for one place, or one time, but for all places and times." D.L. Moody, at San Francisco, Jan. 1st, 1881.

Why does the Day we Keep the Sabbath Matter?

If we break one of the Ten Commandments, God's word says, we are guilty of breaking them all.

"For whosoever shall keep the whole law, and yet offend in one point, he is guilty of all. For he that said, Do not commit adultery, said also, Do not kill. Now if thou commit no adultery, yet if thou kill, thou art become a transgressor of the law." (James 2:10-11).

So, if we neither kill nor commit adultery, but break the Sabbath, we are guilty of breaking all of the commandments, as we are sinners. It also reiterates it in the New Testament book of Matthew 5:18
"For verily I say unto you, Till heaven and earth pass, one jot or one tittle shall in no wise pass from the law, till all be fulfilled."

Sadly, however, most Christian religions believe that the Fourth Commandment has been done away with, but it is important to note that the

Sabbath is called a 'perpetual covenant', meaning a continuing covenant, between God and His people. Nowhere in the Bible does it say that the Sabbath covenant was to come to an end after the resurrection of Christ. Instead, it actually says that it will continue on Earth as well as in Heaven.

"And it shall come to pass, that from one new moon to another, and from one sabbath to another, shall all flesh come to worship before me, saith the LORD." (Isaiah 66:23).

Also, remembering that Jesus, the apostles and the early New Testament church kept the Sabbath, the only conclusion we can come to is that we also should be keeping the Sabbath as God has commanded us to.

APPENDIX I
THE UNSEEN REALM

◉ There have been two events which have happened in my youth which I have not really thought about in detail in my adult life, until my car doors were bent outside my house when I was trying to go to church. Both are sort of opposites of each other and really helped me fathom what was going on in the realm in which we cannot see.

1. This event took place in the city of Leicester, a medium-sized city situated in the East Midlands of England. My father's two brothers and three sisters live there with their families. When I was growing up, we would often visit them, and it was loads of fun because his brothers both had sons the same age as my brother and I. Together we would go exploring around the many warehouses and textile factories that were within walking distance. We would scale the fences and walls and enter the compounds where those buildings were located. Security back then wasn't anything like it is today and access was relatively easy as there was no CCTV. I don't think it occurred to us that we were trespassing and could be prosecuted. As far as we were concerned, it was just a bit of fun and we weren't trying to steal anything or cause any damage. Whether or not our parents or the police would have taken the same view, I doubt very

much.

I remember one day in particular. We woke up and decided to go exploring around another textile manufacturing estate. We had to climb and scale over many obstacles, including roofs, fences and gates, to get through to the secured area. En route was a very high narrow access wall with an incredibly long drop on one side leading to the concrete floor, and a fairly long drop on the other where you could see very old, weathered tiled roofs, attached to abandoned warehouses. Either side wasn't safe at all.

Once in the compound, we just innocently messed around like young kids do. We pretended to drive various machines by sitting on them and generally explored what was about. At some point, after what had been about an hour of playing, we heard a shout. We turned and looked and realised that we were spotted by a security guard. He began to give chase. My cousins and my brother were way back at the safer end. From there they had quick access to the route which we came in so they headed straight back up. As for my other cousin and I, we were cornered and made a swift decision to hide behind a wall. We were there for quite a while, but at least we could keep an eye on the security guard, who had had his eyes on the bigger group, but gave up on them when he realised that they had escaped. After which he slowly made his way back from where he had come.

My cousin and I were a little shaken and worried, but we finally got the confidence to emerge from our hiding place to head back to his home, as we reckoned the others would probably be almost there by that time. However, as we started walking, unbeknown to us, the security guard had returned. It was my cousin who noticed. He heard a noise behind us and turned to look. It was the security guard, being as stealthy as he could, making tracks in our direction, and he was gaining on us. At once, we sprinted, running our hearts out in the direction of the way we came in. We started climbing the fences and made our way up onto the roofs and from there we scaled across and got into a courtyard. Then climbed up a giant gate and got onto the high narrow wall I mentioned earlier. My cousin went first. He wasn't confident on the wall so he sat on his bottom and very slowly shuffled his way along, while I eagerly walked behind him. With the pace he was going and the fear of the security guard, he made me grow very anxious as I urged him to go faster, telling him to stand up and walk to increase his speed. But he wouldn't, he was too scared. Not wishing to wait any longer, as I walked very slowly behind him, waiting and getting very frustrated, I looked down one side of the wall at the sheer drop which led to the ground. It was incredibly high and then I looked down the other side, where there was a shorter drop but which went to the old warehouse roofs. I thought that if I could get onto the roof tiles, I could then just run across them and not have to hang around waiting for my cousin. In an instant, I jumped down onto the roof. Unfortunately, I hadn't taken into account my weight and the age and/or the proper condition of the roof. As my feet hit the tiles, I went crashing straight through into the warehouse, dropping down the same height that was on the other side of the wall, into complete darkness.

I think I must have knocked myself out temporarily because the next thing I was aware of was waking up on my back and looking up to see the hole in the roof where I had fallen through. Apart from that light coming in, the place was pitch-black. I called out to my cousin, but there was no answer. He was long gone; I doubt he'd even realised what had happened.

I tried to remain calm, adjusted my eyes to the gloom and peered around the room. There was nothing in it, and neither was there a way out. I started to panic.

Realising that I had to get out of there fast, in vain, I tried a running jump to see if I could grab the sides of the hole where I fell in, but it was far too high. With desperation and fear overcoming me, I tried again and again, but it was useless. It started to dawn on me the trouble I was in and a feeling of hopelessness started to come over me. No one knew where I was and I was trapped on private property. In panic I decided to look around this empty room again, and I did but the only thing I could see was a very old car tyre. I don't know why but I went and grabbed it and took it over to the hole and tried to stand on it, but because it was soft and narrow, it just caved in then I just wobbled and fell off it. I could see from the light coming through the hole that it was a vintage car tyre. It was the kind that was on cars from the 1960s, like a Ford Anglia, which had seen better times and that it was never going to be strong enough to hold my weight and even if it had, the tyre was nowhere near giving me the height I needed to climb back out. In any case, even if I was able to grab hold of the edges of the tiles, they wouldn't be able to hold me plus they were extremely sharp and jagged. The numberous variables were against me and I started to think about my despair again.

I have no idea why but I then decided to try rolling the tyre slowly under the direction of the hole in the roof, and as it would roll, to then run from another angle and very lightly use it to springboard myself up and grab the edges of the jagged tiles. I couldn't see any way it was going to work, but I had to try something, I rolled it anyway. As I suspected, the attempt ended in failure. The tyre rolled too fast and my whole timing was off. So I tried again, then again but it wasn't working. I stopped for a moment, composed myself. I don't know why but this idea was now branded into my head, I was convinced somehow this was going to work. This time, I decidedly rolled the tyre much more slowly, I took my place at another angle, watching and waiting very patiently for it to just reach the edge of the hole. As it did, I ran as fast as I could towards the tyre jumping very lightly onto it with one foot. When my foot touched the top of the tyre, I felt something grab me under the arms and raise me up out of the hole and place me back onto the wall. I was shocked as I tried to understand what had occurred. But there was no time to hang about and ponder on the moment as the thought of a lurking security guard got me in flight mode again. Explanations would have to wait for later. I quickly regained my senses and headed for my uncle's house as fast as possible. Not wishing to go through a repeat performance of my earlier fall, I sat down and shuffled my way along the wall like my cousin had done so successfully a little while earlier. When I arrived back my brother and all of my cousins were sitting around having dinner. Wondering what had taken me so long, my cousin had thought the security guard had caught me, but little did he or the rest of them know what had really happened.

2. This event took place a few years after the previous one.

It had been quite an evening, but that would count for very little if my father woke up and caught me creeping in at an hour past midnight. So it was with all the covert strategy a fifteen-year-old could gather in an attempt to remain totally silent to even the lightest of sleepers that I started to enter my house. I carefully lined up my key with the door lock and slowly pushed it into place. Then, covering the lock with my other hand to try and further mute the sound, I turned the key, pulled the handle down and gently pushed the door open. I crept in quietly and grabbed hold of the door handle before it could return to its initial resting position with its loudish squeak, a technique my brother and I had got down to a fine art form over the past couple of years, and with said handle firmly in my grip, I silently closed the door, locked it and returned the key to the cupboard drawer in the kitchen. Part one of my mission was complete.

Years of shift work had ruined my dad's ability to get his head down for a solid eight hours and as a result, he was a very light sleeper. I really didn't want to wake him up for two reasons: the first being that he was the stricter parent and the knowledge of me rolling in so late, when I had been due back much earlier would, without a shadow of doubt, lead to me getting into some serious trouble. The second was that my dad had worked ever since he was a very young boy, and so I always had (and still have) the utmost respect for everything he had done to make our household what it was, which in turn meant that I didn't want to do anything to cause unnecessary waves in his life. Also at the time, it was the summer holidays and he was struggling more than ever with the general noise and everyday disruption to the usual household routine, caused by me and my siblings being off school.

My mother had always been a light sleeper too. I never quite understood why at the time, thinking that my father's various shifts may have had a bad effect on her sleeping habits, but looking back and knowing her character, I now fully understand that it was because she had young children in the house and wouldn't allow herself to go into a deep sleep, more so if one of us was ill, out or away.

But returning to that night, I don't think I had ever crept up stairs so slowly in all my life. The late-night silence played havoc with my senses and each and every one of my footsteps, no matter how carefully I put my feet down, seemed to reverberate around the house like a series of mini sonic booms. At least, that was what I was hearing, when in reality, I was very silent.

After what seemed like an age, but was probably no more than four minutes, I finally got to the top of the stairs. I paused briefly, straining my ears to hear if there were sounds of any untoward movement coming from any of the bedrooms. To my utmost relief, all was silent.

My bedroom was on the immediate left. I had shared it with my brother up until a couple of weeks previously, but we had been arguing a lot and so he had switched to sleeping in my sister's room.

I have to hold my hand up and take the blame for that particular circumstance, as sometimes I could be unbearable to be around. I had been very unsettled as a young kid and unlike my siblings, I was completely haywire and needed to be by myself a lot of the time. Even though my brother decamping was only for a trial period, I felt regret that he had been pushed out, although in reality, it was probably a blessing for everyone. In truth, I didn't know what on earth was going on with me and nor could I subdue it. Sometimes my behaviour was out of control. It's really hard to explain. I just couldn't stop myself. I would be nice and pleasant one day, and the next, I would be raging and ranting all over the place, finding arguments and fights and generally being a right pain to anyone who dared come within ten feet of me. My attitude was one of sheer rebellion in whatever I did. I disliked authority and couldn't find long-term peace.

So my brother moving out was the best solution for everyone. I could have my own space and my family wouldn't have to deal with my nonsense. I could get upset by anything, no matter how small or trivial it might be, never being able to shake off the feeling, so in my room, alone, I could vent to my heart's content. I did feel quite lonely at times though, but it was my life's course and I know my brother was well off out of my unpredictability, as I could seriously have had a bad influence on his life.

Anyway, I made my way across the landing to my door, it was only a few steps, but I held my breath and opened and closed my bedroom door in one fell swoop, it was in complete silence. I was in. Stage two complete. Then I turned the light on, using my palm, again as a kind of muting system to deaden the click of the switch. That's the kind of noise you don't pay any attention to during the day, as it gets drowned out by all the other goings-on, but in the dead of night, when the house is absolutely quiet, it somehow seems to amplify itself to a level that is off the charts.

I quickly got into my bed clothes, turned off the light, again with palm muting, and climbed into bed. My eyes immediately adjusted and I was able to observe my small, basic rectangular room with a chest of drawers, a little desk and chair. It was pretty clear, considering it was late, as the light from the streetlamp outside my house penetrated the curtains. I listened carefully for about twenty seconds but heard nothing. Nobody was stirring. I hadn't woken anybody up. Mission accomplished!

Laying in my bed and looking towards my door, I finally got a chance to reflect on the evening I'd spent around Gary's house. The time had flown by so quickly. I'd got there at just after 6.00pm, as I knew he and his family always had their dinner between 5.00pm and that hour. We didn't see as much of each other as we had done when we were younger because we both had both gone to different secondary schools. Consequently, although we tried to meet up as often as we could, we did most of our catching up on the weekends. It wasn't so bad during the summer holidays as we had the whole week to engage with each other. We were both football fanatics and if we weren't outside organizing a match or just having a kick around, we would be watching football on TV or playing a football game on the computer.

That particular evening had been one of playing football on the computer. His father had recently bought a groundbreaking new game, which might not seem much now, but back then it was revolutionary. I recall it being the first of its kind for including every single professional player on the planet, which for the 1990s was an absolutely massive achievement. It was an incredible game, with the possibilities of player purchases etc.

My friend quickly loaded it and we were away. I had to be home by ten o'clock, so we had four glorious hours of game time ahead of us. I was completely wrapped up in my team and they had a real chance of actually winning the league. All the while I tried to keep a close eye on the clock, as my father had made it quite clear to me that I wasn't to stay out too late, but the game was so engrossing that we were well into extra time - about two and a half hours of it - before I realised, much to my shock and horror, that ten o'clock had come and gone and I hadn't even noticed!

While I was pondering on the game and what new player purchases I would be making the following day, someone walked through my bedroom door and stood in the corner of the room. While they stared at me intently I realised something, they had actually walked right through my door, literally through it without any recourse to the handle!

If that surprises you or fills you with alarm, imagine for a moment how I felt as a fifteen-year-old. At first, I thought I was seeing things, but it was happening. I thought it was my mother, although how I thought she'd just materialised in my room at just gone 1.00am in the morning, I don't know. I think I was in such a state of panic and deep trepidation that all semblance of logical thought just waved a white flag. I looked at the apparition for a few seconds and began to feel very frightened and unsettled. I asked who was there, but didn't receive a reply. I attempted to sit up, but found to my surprise that I couldn't! I was physically frozen, and any movement, no matter how slight, was out of the question.

They stood there staring at me and as I peered more closely I could see that whoever it was was wearing a crown. I tried to analyse their face to work out who it was, the best I could, and it was then that I realised that they were not human! Blind panic came in. Eventually working out their face I have to say that it was the most unusual being I have ever seen in my life, very evil and angry-looking, I was petrified! My mood immediately changed, as did the atmosphere in the entire room.

The apparition's features looked grotesque. It was generally black in colour like a shadow, but at the same time, a physical being. Its body seemed to be like a flickering light, but there was no light in it whatsoever. To add to my terror, while I was trying to work things out, something even more alarming happened! Lots more similar beings started walking through my door, surrounding my bed! I can't describe exactly how I felt, other than to say I was paralysed with abject fear and dread. I stopped trying to move and couldn't close my eyes. Those beings continued to flood into my room, filling it up and all looking over me. I was in complete and utter terror. But then the beings allowed the one with the crown to stand over me. It placed its hand over me and started chanting something as the other beings moved around me at speed. It felt as though the room was on fire, but that was in fact due to their flickering and rapid movement, plus they seemed to be carrying a very evil and negative aura. Needless to say, I couldn't comprehend what was happening and I found myself unable to internally articulate any coherent thoughts.

After what was about five minutes (but seemed like a much longer period of time), the beings eventually stopped what they were doing and left the room one by one, with the leader departing midway. When the final one had gone, I quickly became aware that once more I could move. I jumped out of my bed and put my light on, but I was so scared of even being by the door, I opened it and went out into the hallway, putting that light on as well. Then I stood outside my parents' bedroom, trying to get myself together as I reflected on what had just happened. My hand was on their door handle but I didn't turn it or go in, and looking back, I must have been standing outside their room for about an hour.

I think the reason I didn't go in was because I was having grave doubts as to whether or not they would believe me. *What would happen if I told them? What would they say? Would they be angry that I'd woken them up with what they perceive as some half-baked fantasy? They would probably say that I had had a nightmare.* There were just so many factors stopping me from just waking them up and screaming out what had happened, that in the end, I think it was my rebellious attitude that won the day.

Having decided not to go in, I then took a step back and thought about what I was going to do next. I was too scared to go back into my room and it took a lot of talking myself round before I finally plucked up the courage to open the door again and make sure the light was on. It was. I peeked in cautiously and assured myself that I was alone. I then slipped in and stood by the door for a while, worried sick. At that moment, I thought I couldn't face the rest of the night, so I decided to stay awake and wait until everyone got up in the morning, which was still several hours away. *Perhaps it had all been a dream. Maybe I had been seeing things. No, I couldn't accept that reasoning. I knew what had happened, and although it defied all logic (that I knew), it had been real, and it would be even more insane to dismiss it.*

After another inordinate length of time just standing and thinking by the light switch with the door open, I figured I couldn't remain where I was all night and that the best way to deal with the situation was to get back into bed.

I psyched myself ready, and acting on pure adrenaline, I jumped into my bed, got under the cover and stayed there for bit. As I lay under the covers, getting hotter by the minute, scary thoughts carried on running through my mind. *What was outside the covers, if anything?* There was no way I had the confidence to check, so I stayed where I was, trying not to move. After some time, I realised that the light was still on and annoyingly having a disposition of being "green" for the planet I just had to turn it off. I decided to turn it off as swiftly as I could, which I did. Now I was back where I was, laying there in the foetal position terrified, thinking about the demons, hoping they were gone and wondering who they were, why they had come and how on earth anyone would believe me. At some point in the dead of the night with thoughts racing in my mind, exhausted from the days' play and recent events, I must have drifted off.

It was light. Morning had arrived. I was safe! I was still feeling very spooked, so I got up fast and made my way downstairs faster than usual. I knew everyone was up because I could hear their voices coming up from the kitchen. As I got to my living room only my dad was there, I couldn't keep it to myself so I had to tell my father what had happened. As I related my experience, he just shrugged it off and said that I must have been seeing things and the best thing I could do would be to ignore it and move on. I was really annoyed with him responding like that but after some thought I realised that all I could do was just that.

In the months that followed, after the visitation, I realised that the impact that was left on me was huge. I was sure of what I saw but kept it to myself from then on because I knew that people simply wouldn't believe a fifteen-year-old kid's story of this kind. I also noticed that I had developed the habit of sleeping with my head under the covers, at least for a couple of months until I was in the place where I was sure they wouldn't come again.

At the time of the event, I thought my father hadn't taken me very seriously and that he hadn't listened to me properly, but it wasn't until a few years later that I got more of a satisfactory response.

A conversation about supernatural things had come up between my father and his best friend, who was an Italian Roman Catholic. They were talking about the worldwide apparitions of Mary etc. My father nodded agreeing with him that these things existed, and even contributed a supernatural story of his own, which he had experienced in Africa. That really annoyed and frustrated me, especially when I cast my mind back to my father's reaction to my story, so I decided to speak about my experience to my dad's friend.

His reaction was quite different. He didn't disbelieve my experience for one moment and said that those things are always present in the unseen realm.

Later in time I told my mother about this event also, and mentioned that my father hadn't believed me. She went on to tell me that one of his elderly relatives was involved black magic and she believed that my dad was protecting me by not focusing on negative things as these. I didn't press the matter any further.

****

"The Sabbath will be the great test of loyalty, for it is the point of truth especially controverted. When the final test shall be brought to bear upon men, then the line of distinction will be drawn between those who serve God and those who serve Him not. While the observance of the false sabbath in compliance with the law of the state, contrary to the fourth commandment, will be an avowal of allegiance to a power that is in opposition to God, the keeping of the true Sabbath, in obedience to God's law, is an evidence of loyalty to the Creator. While one class, by accepting the sign of submission to earthly powers, receive the mark of the beast, the other choosing the token of allegiance to divine authority, receive the seal of God." (White, E G, Pacific Press Publishing Association, 1950, *The Great Controversy*, p.605)

****

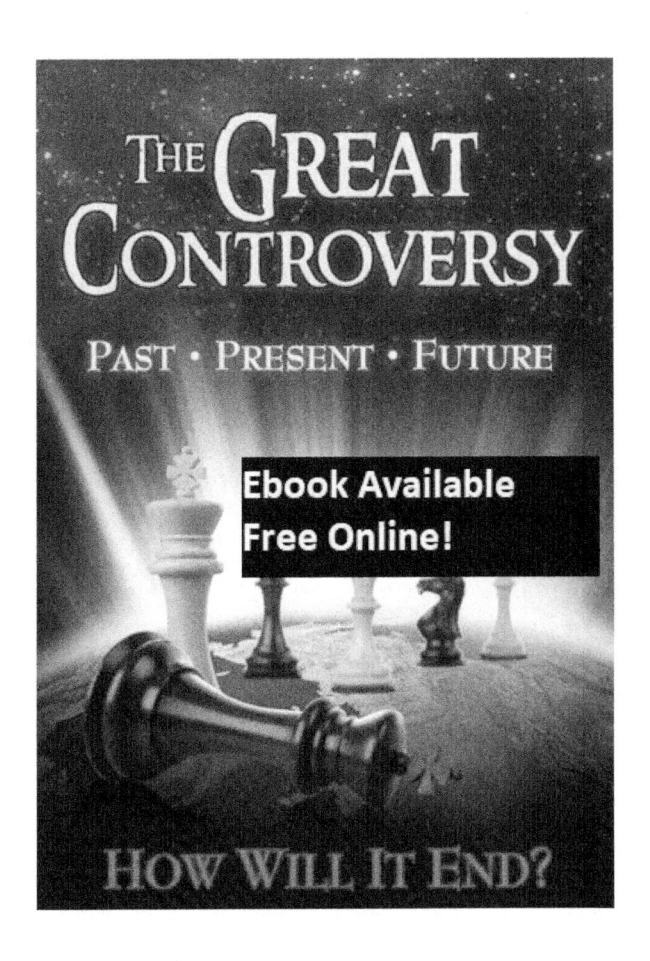

THE GREAT CONTROVERSY

PAST · PRESENT · FUTURE

Ebook Available Free Online!

HOW WILL IT END?

AN OPEN LETTER

Dear friend,

Thank you for taking the time out to read about my life. I hope you have enjoyed reading it as much as I have enjoyed writing it. I am sincerely hoping that you have been stirred up to make an enquiry into what I am saying within this book.

Sadly, some people who are hardened-hearted may find my true stories and the factual evidence I have presented as offensive, to which I genuinely apologise. In Jesus' time people were very offended by Him presenting facts, however the truth stands by itself and in the same way as Him, all I can do is share what I have learned along the journey of my life with complete transparency.

This is a genuine and friendly plea to take a moment to note the RECOMMENDED RESOURCES coming up in this book, as well as the things mentioned in the appendices, owe it to yourself that you are fully convicted as to where you stand in life.

Take some time to work out whether I have presented the truth. Do it the educated way and not the dismissive way. You owe it to yourself and your family.

May God bless you!
Bav

RECOMMENDED RESOURCES

Books:
The Great Controversy – Ellen G White

Seeking Allah Finding Jesus: A Devout Muslim Encounters Jesus
– Nabeel Qureshi (**Muslim**)
The Richest Caveman – Doug Batchelor (**Jewish**)
Found by Love: A Hindu Priest Encounters Jesus
– Rahil Patel (**Hindu**)
Deceived by the New Age – Will Baron (**New Age**)

Online Videos:
A Trip into the Supernatural – Roger Morneau (**Satanist**)
From Evolutionist to Creationist – Walter Veith (**Atheist**)
Testimony – Mark Cleminson (**Member of the Illuminati**)
Testimony – Clifford Goldstein (**Jewish**)
*The Testimony of a Former **Zen Buddhist*** - Yip Kok Tho
Testimony – Mark Finley (**Catholic**)
*Testimony of a Former **Baptist** Pastor* - Quinton Smith
Testimony – Mark Martin (**Jehovah's Witness**)

Testimony – Angus T Jones (**TV Celebrity**)
Escape from the Black Hole – Ivor Myers (**Musician/Rapper**)

Online Presentations:
Total Onslaught – Walter Veith
Come Search with Me, Let's Look for God - Subodh Pandit
God's Final Call – Mark Woodman

Websites:
https://www.amazingfacts.org
https://egwwritings.org/
http://www.sabbathtruth.com/
http://amazingdiscoveries.org
https://www.audioverse.org

A SPECIAL THANKS TO:

DON WARD
JOSEPH & JUDI QUINTANA
NICOLA DICKINSON
LARRY LEISTER
JANICE BAILEY
SALPY KASPARIAN
MANDY ATKINS
SALMA WILIKAI
MICHAEL PUPOVAC
ROMAN SELIVANOV
GREG SEREDA (FROM BIBLE FLOCK BOX)
GARTH & ALETA BAINBRIDGE
TIMOTHY FORDHAM
BINDY BEGG
MARK & YVONNE LONDON

THE DARK VISITOR

"THIS BOOK IS AN ACTUAL ACCOUNT THAT EXPOSES THE EXTREME LENGTHS SATAN WILL GO TO IN ORDER TO DECEIVE PEOPLE FROM KNOWING GOD'S TRUTHS"

For further information email :
SURETYSEVEN@OUTLOOK.COM

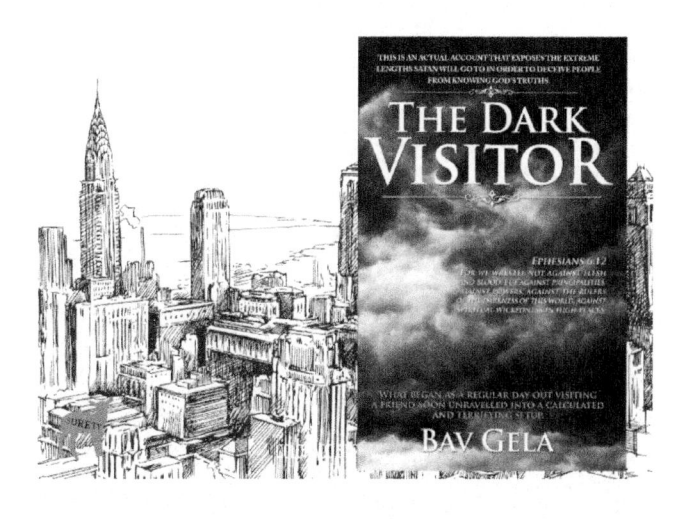

AMAZING FACTS
FREE ONLINE
BIBLE SCHOOL
https://www.amazingfacts.org/bible-study/free-online-bible-school

Printed in Great Britain
by Amazon